Stop Being a Bitch

and

Get a Boyfriend

The Best Advice I Finally Took

By

Gina Hendrix

Stop Being a Bitch and Get a Boyfriend

© 2011 Gina Hendrix

~ *Table of Contents* ~

INTRODUCTION

First, let's debunk the myth that men love bitches. They DO NOT!

I have had the privilege of getting this inside information straight from the horse's mouth—my male clients. As a matchmaker, I work with the most eligible, handsome, and sought after men. And guess what? They tell me *everything*. To be honest with you, sometimes it can be very hard to hear what they have to say about what women do that turns them off. A lot of the time, I can identify with what the girl was doing! Let me tell you, my matchmaking business has been, and continues to be, an eye opening experience from *every* angle.

My advice here is a combination of what I've learned from my matchmaking business and what I know that I've personally done wrong in the dating world.

This book is geared towards women and is focused on the things that they do in spite of themselves in the dating world. Don't get me wrong—men aren't perfect either. But, in an effort to get you what you want, for the purpose of this book, I'm only focused on helping my ladies change their ways.

This book is designed to be honest (as if I were shaking you by the shoulders saying, "Come on, Girl!!!") and to hopefully be a wake-up call. I really do want you to be happy. So, let me be clear: when I use the term "bitch" in this book, it's tongue in cheek. It's really used as a way to get your attention and make the subject matter more lighthearted. Really, you could easily swap the phrase "being a bitch" in the title for a variety of other behaviors we all slip into from time to time—*Stop Being Irrational and Get a Boyfriend, Stop Being Needy and Get a Boyfriend*, stop nagging, stop being obsessive, stop being bossy... you see what I mean?

And it's not just you. I'll admit that I, too, have been there and done that! I've been many of the girls in this book—not *all*, but many. And if you make the mistakes that I've made and that I've seen many other women make, then you're probably still single. The truth is, you won't get a boyfriend, a husband, or any man to stick around for very long if you keep repeating your old habits that I discuss in the book. I'm hoping that if you're reading this book, you will learn from these common mistakes and from the many stories that fill the pages here. I'm really hoping that you will listen, learn, and start doing things a little differently.

I know most relationship advice books tend to handle us ladies with kid gloves, but if you're like me, you might be too hard headed. With this book, my book, the book I'm writing to myself as well as to you, I'm going to give it to you straight—no kid gloves here. If you don't have a boyfriend and you want one, well, my friend, it's time we had an honest talk...

Take it from me—men *do not* like bitches!

CHAPTER 1:

Which Bitch Are You?

Welcome, welcome! Please, drop your tickets in the ticket box and enter the Bitchy Fun House of Potential Terror! Look around our vast tent of mirrors and see visions of what you will become under the influence of the minds and behaviors of our gallery of bitches! Please, by all means, take a gander!

First, behold the **All-Business Bitch**, where your flirty feminine side is (POOF!) gone and left in its place is a cold, aloof, successful businesswoman. She's out to meet the world, but not a boyfriend! Of course, it's hard to say whether that's better or worse when you stand in front of the next mirror. (Hint: neither is good.)

See yourself as a **Freaky Bitch,** and all of a sudden, your good judgment is out the window. The next thing you know, you'll be like those celebrities who forget to wear their panties in public.

Moving right along... oh, now this is a shame. Linger in front of the **Insecure Bitch** mirror too long, and you'll instantly be too thin, too fat, too tall, or too short. Yikes! That's no good, and neither is this! Stand before the **Picky Bitch** mirror, and you'll be ruling out every man that walks by you, in favor of your fantasy man— who never appears.

Step on down to the **Obsessive Bitch** mirror, where your mind will be racing with nothing but thoughts of HIM, all of the time. And just you wait, my friend! This tent holds only a small preview of the myriad of "bitches" you're about to meet!

Spooky, isn't it? Spookier still is that for each mirror in this tent, there's a real, live version of that girl walking around in the world, destructing her relationships by letting herself be seduced by these self-defeating habits. There's a good chance that some of these "bitches" have caught up with you, too, at one time or another, and under her spell, you've self-sabotaged your best efforts to land a boyfriend. These bitches will make you do things that a nice, normal girl like you wouldn't normally do!

So, now that you've taken a spin around the fun house, do you have a sense of which "bitch" you might be? If not, don't fret. We have plenty of options, and there's plenty to learn. Through self-reflective tests, personal experiences, and stories I've collected along the way, I'm going to shed some light on what you've been doing, what I've done, and what I've seen other women do.

We're also going to have a little fun, laughing at each of these "bitches" and, in a sense, at ourselves. These easy-to-slip-into behaviors have haunted each of us from time to time. Luckily for us, though, these bad habits, or "bitches," don't have to be permanent. By the end of this book, you're going to say goodbye to the bitch and hello to your new boyfriend!

CHAPTER 2:

All-Business Bitch

Brrr... it's frosty in here. Did you just feel that gust of cold air? It's chilling everything from the conversation to—whoops! A draft just went up your skirt. Now *that's* ice-cold too!

And what's causing this deep freeze, you ask? It's simple: while you were out succeeding in business, you put your sexuality on ice. Now, it's time to thaw it out and warm up your love life. The only thing that should be on ice is a bottle of bubbly reserved for you and that supremely sexy man you would be with right now, if your mind and libido weren't so frostbitten by your need to succeed in business.

There's a very famous line from the film *Working Girl* that goes like this: "I have a head for business and a bod for sin!" Right now you only have a head for business, so let's get you in the mood to sin!

You might be so frozen that you don't even realize your lady parts are about to fall off. Has All-Business Bitch stolen your sexuality?

❖ <u>**All-Business Alert—Take the TEST!**</u>

Pardon me, but will you please adjust your glasses, sit up straight, and take a moment of your time to answer some of the following questions:

- Do you have trouble leaving the businesswoman at the office?
- Do you feel happiest when talking about work?
- These days, is *sexy* the last thing on your mind?
- Don't even get me started on your collection of lingerie—do you just call it "underwear," and your main qualification for whether or not to buy it is if it'll be "comfortable for work?"
- Are you oblivious to men when they try to flirt with you?
- Have you forgotten how to flirt?
- Is your idea of getting to know someone asking them about their 401K or what accountant they use?

Turning a date into business mentoring session might help you in business, but it isn't going to help you get a boyfriend. This is NOT a meeting! Please, please read on. All work and no play make for many lonely nights at home with take-out and your computer!

✠ Kelly

Kelly had always been an achiever. Now, in her early thirties, she was a successful attorney, and she was close to making partner at her firm.

Of course, such success required an extreme level of focus from Kelly. She worked at least six days a week, sometimes seven. The days that she worked, she was working at least twelve hours a day and often times even more. Because Kelly didn't have anyone waiting for her at home, she found it very hard to pull herself away from her computer and much easier to just keep working.

Now that Kelly was rather successful, she had started to think about her overall future. She saw the sand running out of the hourglass quickly. She wanted a husband and children—a family. Kelly was a great girl with a lot to offer, and once she made her mind up to achieve a goal, that was that. So she now decided to put all of her effort into her "man plan," and she kicked it into full gear by asking friends to set her up if they knew of anyone great.

Kelly's best friend, Kate, set her up on a date with her husband's good friend, Tom. Tom was a handsome, smart, successful entrepreneur, and Kate was sure he and Kelly would hit it off. Kelly and Tom set a date to meet for lunch on a Saturday afternoon. Kelly had even taken the entire day off for the date, at the suggestion of Kate.

"You need to have fun once in awhile!" Kate had said.

Kate was right; Kelly did need to have fun sometimes. Unfortunately, Kelly had forgotten how. Through her law firm, Kelly encountered so many men to whom she had to put on a professional appearance that Kelly had put her sexy, flirty self on the back burner and regarded almost everyone she met as a potential business contact. This was all too apparent when she got to her date with Tom.

When they met for their date, Kelly immediately thought Tom was extremely handsome, and from her perspective, their date went pretty well—there was constant conversation. However, Kelly was fuelling most of the conversation, and she was asking Tom the kinds of questions that she might ask someone with whom she was having a networking lunch. "So do you have an MBA?" "I read an article recently about the new tax laws going into effect here in Oregon, did you read it?" "I just moved my 401K to an IRA; what's your opinion on that?"

Finally, at the end of the lunch, right before he turned to leave, Kelly asked the most businesslike question of all. "Oh, I almost forgot!

Who does your taxes? I've been looking for a new accountant for awhile. Do you have anyone that you would recommend?"

There was an awkward pause. Before answering, Tom stared blankly at Kelly as though to say, *Really?!*

All in all, the date itself went fine, but nevertheless, Tom didn't call Kelly for another date.

His View

"Kelly was great. She was really nice and friendly. She was all business, though. With the types of things we talked about, I didn't really feel like it was a date or had any romantic potential. She seems really focused, and she's probably a great attorney, though. She knows her stuff. I'd recommend her to anyone who needs some good legal advice."

The Reality

Kelly WAS NOT looking for another client! She was looking for a boyfriend!

Because Kelly was so focused on her job, she had let it take over her life. She had gotten to the point where just about everything in her day revolved around "shop talk." And because she was never *not* in business mode, Kelly regarded Tom the way she would a business associate or someone at a networking event: as a source of information and opportunity. Tom may have indeed been a great source of information and opportunity, but that wasn't why he and Kelly were having lunch. They had lunch to connect, to get to know one another, and to potentially date.

Though they come in similar packages (meeting with a stranger, usually over a meal), business meetings and dates are absolutely 100% not the same thing. Where a business meeting is a networking opportunity, a date is an opportunity to get to know the personal side of someone. Business meetings are for relaying information, showing your high intellect, and impressing them with your negotiation skills. Dates are for letting your guard down and your hair hang loose. It's a time to let your fun, feminine side show through, by sharing your personal interests and being open.

The trouble is, if you've been single a long time and your career has become your boyfriend, it can be a challenge to switch gears. But, you must! It's crucial to having a relationship. The same way you wouldn't send a flirty, party girl on a job interview, sending the All-Business Bitch on a first date probably won't get her the job of being a girlfriend. Sexy, single girls get taken out, whereas the All-Business Bitch just takes meetings. Got it?

Your job can be very special to you, but nevertheless, matters of business are anything but sexy, fun, and flirty. Think about it: did you ever make a friend at work? Probably. What's the biggest indicator that a person has gone from colleague to friend? In my experience, someone becomes a friend when we stop talking about work and start talking about things that are going on in our personal lives. Work isn't personal; it's work. Families, hobbies, outside interests—that's what makes up who we really are—who our friends and potential spouses know and love.

I understand your intelligence can be something you want to show off because you're proud it, but believe me, men will not ask you on a second date because you knew what the closing stock market prices were. You're on top of the world at work, and because you've let yourself get so wrapped up in it and be defined so much by it, to you, your workplace achievement is your most winning quality. In reality, you've got a lot more going on than being a top dog at the office. You're fun. You're flirty. You're funny. You're smart. Right?

If you are trying to find a committed relationship, make a commitment to yourself that you are going to focus on your personal life with the same passion that you pour into your professional life. Just like a career, relationships take work, and so does finding one! When you have dates, remember to leave your job and all of the business-like thinking (and talking) that goes with it at the office and let the sexy out! And since you've been working so hard lately, it may take some practice to get that Sexy Bitch back—so coax her away from the computer and then stand back and let her loose! A girls' day out, with shopping, cocktails, and a hair and make-up session is definitely in order!

Do something every day that is sexy and flirty. Flirt with the checkout guy at the grocery store, if you have to! Bring sexy back. Buy yourself something sexy that you normally would never wear, and throw on some SUPER sexy lingerie. Read a racy romance novel. Flirt with the mailman or your cute new neighbor. Why not? Remind yourself that although you are a savvy businesswoman by day, you need to be sexy minx by night! Think of it as exercise or logging practice hours. Build your girly muscle mass.

Once you've mastered the art of being feminine and flirtatious on dates, you'll be able to close the most important deal of all.

CHAPTER 3:

Bitter Bitch

Ugh! Do you feel that negativity? It's draining the energy from my life. Suddenly, it's like anything I say or do is met with criticism and doubt. That's strange. I didn't start feeling it until you got here. Hmmmmm. Is it a mystery, or could it be you? Well, let's just see. Please, allow me to seat you at your table so that you can answer a few important questions. We're going to get to the bottom of this once and for all. Come this way, Bitter, Party of One!

❖ Bitter Alert—Take the TEST!

Could this *possibly,* just *possibly,* be you?

- Is blaming others your favorite past time?
- Is your mantra "There are just no good men out there, anywhere"?
- Can you not wait to meet your date, just so you can prove to yourself that your mantra is true?

- Is complaining your drink of choice?
- Are suspicion and doubt your best friends?
- Is your nickname "Why me?"

Uh-oh! Were you just settling in with your best friends, "suspicion and doubt," for another round of "complaining" on the rocks and a game of "blaming others?" Well, trust me when I say that if you're crowding your mental space with all of that negativity all of the time, then it's virtually impossible for you to ever see the bright side. You do remember the bright side, right? That was the place that you used to frequent before you became a Bitter Bitch. The bright side is that place where everything looks great and the good options are plentiful. And guess what? Here is a secret that you don't know: ALL of the good men are over there on the bright side. That might be why you haven't found one yet.

✠ <u>Kyla</u>

Kyla was at a bit of a crossroads in her life. She had just ended a long reign at an office job that she found to be entirely miserable, and she had started a new gig in an entirely different field at the make-up counter in a very posh department store. Though she had hoped that the job switch would be life changing and would solve her problem of feeling like she was in a rut, she was wary of this new job too. Since she was revamping her work life, she felt she might as well revamp her love life too.

Kyla had a few boyfriends when she was in her 20's, but now that she was in her early 30's, her attitude about life and dating had changed. Kyla felt that things hadn't been going "her way" for a while now. Though her friends always had boyfriends or were going out on dates, Kyla never found anyone very interesting. She told her friend Casey that she felt lonely and really wanted to try to make more of an effort to meet someone soon.

Casey, who had been with her boyfriend for a long time, didn't know too much about the actual dating scene. But, she'd seen many friends have success with online dating sites, so she suggested that to Kyla.

"Ugh. I don't know," Kyla said. "That costs money. I never have any money. I have so many bills to pay off."

Casey brought up the fact that there were actually a few free dating sites, and Kyla responded with, "Yeah, but I bet the guys on those sites are lame and cheap."

Although Casey thought maybe she just shouldn't even bother giving Kyla more suggestions, part of her desperately wanted Kyla to get a boyfriend. Casey was always uncomfortable confiding in Kyla about anything having to do with her own boyfriend because Kyla would always remark with something like, "At least you HAVE a boyfriend!" So, Casey told Kyla that she had read in a magazine about a new hot, super popular dating site that did cost money but that also had a huge great selection of very cute guys. Even if it cost a little money, if Kyla found "The One," it'd be worth it in the long run anyway, right?

That night, when Kyla got home, she went to the site that Casey suggested. She looked around and did in fact see tons of cute guys, so she decided to bite the bullet and pay the monthly fee to check it out. She filled out her profile, and within a couple of days, she started getting a lot of messages from guys who were interested in meeting her. It took quite a few before Kyla was willing to meet one, though; all of the guys that messaged her either weren't good looking enough, weren't tall enough, were too old, were too young, or they just weren't up to Kyla's "standards." After several weeks, she decided to go on a date with a guy named Mike. He was tall and handsome, and he appeared to be just Kyla's "type."

Kyla and Mike were to meet at a bar that was somewhat central for both of them. Kyla arrived frazzled, though, because she hit traffic on her way there. *Of course,* she thought. *The one night I go out, there's going to be traffic. We should have gone somewhere closer to me.* Kyla was even more disappointed when she walked in the door. Mike, who said in his profile that he was six feet tall, was more like five foot ten. He was cute, but he had a weird cowlick in the front of his hair, which made Kyla decide that he wasn't quite as cute as she had expected. Plus, he ordered white wine. *What kind of man orders white wine?* she thought to herself.

Kyla ended the date early, by simply saying, "I'm sorry, but I have to leave." With that, she left Mike sitting there with his white wine.

As soon as she got in her car, she dialed Casey's number. "Oh, my God! Why did I let you talk me into going on that dating site? Ugh! That date was just *awful.* The guy was too short. He was not cute, *and* he ordered white wine. This is such a waste of time! I'm taking myself off that site as soon as I get home. There aren't any good guys on it."

Awkwardly enough for Kyla, about two months later, she was at her new job at the make-up counter when she saw a VERY cute guy approaching. She thought, *Please let him be shopping for his mother!*

When the guy got to her counter, she thought she recognized him, but she wasn't sure how she knew him. Just as she said, "Hi, may I help you?" she placed him. He had a much better haircut, and for some reason, he looked taller and cuter than she remembered.

"Mike?" she asked, surprised. "It's Kyla. We met awhile back from that online site."

Mike looked down and hesitated. Just as he was about to say hi, a tall beautiful blond walked up, kissed him and said, "There you are! You found my favorite make-up counter. I knew you would." And so, Mike introduced Kyla to his new girlfriend, Tammi.

After they made their purchase and left, Kyla thought to herself, *Man, what was I thinking? He was so cute, how did I miss that?*

Too bad for Kyla, but that ship had sailed.

His View

"She was kind of cold, honestly. She showed up fifteen minutes late, which is no big deal to me, but she came in huffing and puffing about the traffic, her job, and how I should have chosen a better location to meet. I told her it was no big deal and tried to make conversation with her. She seemed bored, and before I had even finished my drink, she said she had to go. It was really awkward, and I just kind of sat there, wondering what had happened and if I had done something wrong. About a week later, I met Tammi on the same site, and we've been together ever since."

The Reality

There's a lot going on here, but first, before we can get to the meat of the issue, let's get one thing out of the way first. Why was Kyla calling Casey and blaming her for this botched date? How was it Casey's fault that Kyla joined a dating site on her own, was overly particular on the site, and then didn't really even give the guys a chance? Here's how: Kyla blames other people for her own self-created drama. She doesn't take any accountability for her own actions or the fact that the world doesn't actually owe her anything, nor do her friends or any guys she "graces with her presence."

The only person responsible for Kyla is Kyla. If there's a chance there will be traffic on the way to a date, Kyla should leave a few minutes early, instead of assuming the world is out to get her when she hits traffic. If Kyla joins a dating site, Kyla joins a dating site—not the innocent friend who told her about the site's existence.

Another major problem at foot here was that Mike could tell right away when he met Kyla that she had a negative outlook on life. He didn't call it that, but he sensed it, right? The first thing he said was, *"She was kind of cold, honestly."* Not surprising. Contrary to popular bitter belief, guys are not stupid. They sense vibes right away; the same way that women with their "intuitions" do.

The bitter girl is actually one of the only girls in this book that outside of this book, people might actually refer to as "a bitch." She's miserable, and she puts all of her wretched angst on everyone she knows. She's incapable of seeing the good in any situation; even if she won the lottery, she'd complain about paying the taxes. She blames others for her issues, and she thinks the entire world is out to get her. No matter how hard people try, they can never really connect with her about their lives, because any good news they have to share with her will be met on deaf (and self-absorbed) ears. She thinks everyone should be just as miserable as she is, and she is oblivious that her situations are of her own making.

I was in a store once, and at the register, next to the phone, there was a little handwritten sign, which said "Smile! Customers can hear it!" I laughed a little at this, but it actually is really true. A lot about your attitude and your physical status is revealed through your expressions. What you're experiencing at your core is expressed in every fiber of you from your facial expression to the wrinkles in your forehead to the tone in your voice. And while you're fine festering in your energy of being "left out" of everything good in a glass-half-empty world, there's going to come a day when you meet a guy that you actually like. When you do, guess what? You're not suddenly going to be able to ditch your bitter vibe. It's still going to be there, looming in the background. It's going to be in the tone of your voice; it's going to be in your mannerisms; it's going to be in your facial expressions. A Bitter Bitch doesn't turn into Little Miss Sunshine with the flip of a switch.

The thing is this: if you are bitter, chances are that unless you're willing to completely change your outlook on your life and shed the nasty attitude, you're going to be the same gloomy person you are now a year from now, five years from now, ten years from now, and beyond.   And the even sadder truth is that as long as you're in a negative place, you're probably going to stay single.   It's not because you're not pretty; it's not because you're not smart. It's because you're cynical; you're a defeatist; you're gloomy; and let's face it, you're a bitch.

So, the ONLY way to stop being the soul sucker that you're being is to open your eyes and acknowledge it. You must take responsibility for your life and your attitude. And if you have to, fake it! Fake it! Fake it! *Act* nice and *act* positive, even if it kills you. *Pretend* that you're happy for your friends when they're happy. *Pretend* that you're looking for the positives in the men you date. Why? Because once you start to see all of the positive, wonderful things that will start happening around you, you won't have to fake it anymore. You'll see that with a little positivity, your friendships and you love life will change for the better.

Finally, let's answer Kyla's question about Mike. She asked herself, *How did I miss that?* Well, we know why she missed it, don't we? She missed an opportunity with Mike because she showed up with a negative attitude, and it clouded everything she saw. She was so bitter that she had convinced herself nothing good could ever happen to her. That made her negative about online dating, her job, and even the traffic. She was so negative in life that she subconsciously *expected* to be disappointed, and therefore, she was not able to see Mike in a positive light. But, when she was in a different mental space and he walked up with a clean slate as a guy she thought she didn't know, without any preconceived notions, she saw him as tall and very cute. He was the exact same guy he was on that date; it was Kyla who was different.

If you are of the opinion that "woe is me" and that the universe is out to get you, the truth is that nothing will ever work out for you. It's not because the universe *is* out to get you, though; it's because *you're* out to get you. Your attitude, not luck or a lack thereof, is the cloud looming over your head, pouring a consistent downpour of negativity on you and everyone around you. No one wants to fall victim to your bitterness, and nobody wants to date it, either.

When it comes down to it, it's ALL in your MIND. Life is about *you* and how *you* choose to see it!

CHAPTER 4:
Bossy Bitch

Uh-oh! Did Bossy Pants just walk in? Suddenly, I feel like everything needs to be planned perfectly, and there are a lot of opinions that aren't my own floating around. Whoa! Did you just hear that? I think somebody's restaurant suggestion got killed and replaced with a different one! Oh! Was that YOU who just said the restaurant your date suggested wasn't good enough? Yikes! Um, I think you might just be a Bossy Bitch. I mean, did you really just tell a man where to take you on a date?

❖ Bossy Alert—Take the TEST!

Answer the following questions to see if this sounds like you:

- Are you always on a strict schedule?
- Do you have to have everything perfect?
- Are you thrown by spontaneity?

- Do you rearrange other people's things because you like it better that way?

- Have you ever used a friend's bathroom and replaced the toilet paper roll to go the direction that you prefer?

- When helping others plan events do you end up "taking over" and micro-managing every detail?

Okay, Diva, you need to relax, listen and learn. Here we go!

Bossy bitches will attempt to control every aspect of their lives, from where their friends get together to what food is served at big family dinners. Women who lead and take charge also tend to be very ambitious. And usually, because of their ambition and success, bossy women often want men who are equal to them in every way: they want a man who's in control. A CEO married to a CEO—two bosses, one household—would be picture perfect; wouldn't it?

Unfortunately for you, though, the reality is that the type of guy that you like because he is in charge and powerful, rarely wants to be with a woman who is also "the boss." So, to make it work, you've either got to lose the balls you've grown, or find a guy who's willing to lose his. You can't both be in total control of everything; you'll never get anywhere!

�֎ **Jackie**

Jackie was a "Type A" personality in every way. She was competitive and ambitious, and most of all, she was a planner. As the CEO of a company, Jackie was always the one offering restaurant suggestions to clients, deciding what the game plan was for meetings and defining business strategies. Jackie was a decision maker, and she wanted a man just like her—on top of his world and ready to take charge. Together, they'd be a power couple.

While at a big meeting one day, Jackie got to talking to the CEO of a client company, and they really hit it off. His name was William. Being attracted to his stature as much as his good looks and winning personality, Jackie was very excited when he asked if she would like to have dinner with him sometime.

Jackie and William called two days later and he asked her if she'd like to have dinner the following Thursday night. Jackie said sure, and William suggested that they go to a restaurant called Mirage.

Mirage? thought Jackie after she got off the phone. The last time she was there the crowd was older and the food was dry. *Maybe it's changed...* she thought, as she opened up Yelp and began searching for reviews. They were fairly positive—apparently, the place was under new management—but nevertheless, Jackie couldn't shake her previous impression of it. She couldn't stand the thought of the date going south because of this restaurant choice.

She had recently heard about a great new restaurant in a beautiful hotel across town, so she picked up the phone and called William back. "William? I was thinking—what if we went to the new restaurant at The Plaza Hotel on Thursday instead of Mirage?"

William was a little confused by her suggestion, but nevertheless, he said that he was happy to go to The Plaza Hotel. He suggested that they meet at 8 p.m.

Jackie paused for a moment. "Hmmm," said Jackie, "eight is a little late. Can we do 7:30?"

William said fine, and the date was set: 7:30 p.m. at The Plaza Hotel.

Jackie and William's date was rocky from the start. When Jackie arrived at the restaurant, she saw William sitting at the bar. She waved to him and made her way to the hostess station, where she stated her name.

Confused, William came over to greet her and said, "Our table is all set; I reserved a table in the back for us."

Jackie laughed, and the hostess looked at William and Jackie, confused. Jackie explained that when she suggested the restaurant, she went ahead and made a reservation in her name. The hostess, Jackie, and William all shared an awkward laugh as the hostess showed them to the table that William reserved for the date.

When the wine list was placed on the table in front of William, Jackie craned her neck and asked if she could take a peek. So William acquiesced and handed her the wine list.

While she was gazing down the list, William cleared his throat and asked if she preferred red or white? She said she liked big bold reds, so William suggested that they order a Cabernet or Bordeaux.

"Hmmmm," Jackie said as she continued to consider the list at large, despite William's suggestion. "How about a bottle of Pinot Noir instead?"

The bottle of Pinot was ordered, and Jackie was as happy as a schoolgirl.

Jackie found William incredibly attractive, and his accolades were quite a winning quality for her. The more he talked about his work and all that he had accomplished, the more Jackie fell for him. She was excited to be out with someone who spoke as passionately about his work as she did.

Just after their meals had been served, Jackie began to talk about a mutual business contact that they had both dealt with recently. Jackie found the person to be difficult, and she said so to William.

William said, "Well, I don't know if he's difficult; he just employs a different approach than most."

Jackie held up her hand and cut William off. "William, he's difficult. If you don't realize that, you're wrong. The guy shouldn't even be in business."

After Jackie shut William up about their shared contact, William changed the subject in an attempt to steer clear of work-related conversation.

Toward the end of their dinner, Jackie suggested that she and William grab a drink to continue their date, but he said it was getting late and that he'd better be getting home.

Jackie never got another date with William.

Disappointed by William's rejection, Jackie didn't waste any time before she started to make excuses for why it hadn't gone well. *He must have been threatened by my career. He is probably intimidated by me, and I bet he usually only dates younger girls.*

His View

"Other than saying yes to getting dinner with me, Jackie wasn't willing to say yes to anything I suggested. The restaurant, the time we were to meet, the wine— she clearly wanted it all her way.

When we sat down to dinner, she immediately took charge. I'm surprised that she didn't order my meal for me. When she cut me off while we were talking about a mutual contact and told me that my impression of him was flat out wrong, I saw the forest through the trees.

Jackie likes to spar and be in control. In her mind, she's always right, and there's no discussion of anything, except what she wants or thinks. I work too hard and my job is demanding enough. When I'm not working, I want to enjoy life and relax. With Jackie, I felt like I was with one of the guys from the office, and that is NOT what I'm looking for in a woman."

The Reality

Jackie turned William off for sure, but it wasn't because she was too old or too smart. Instead, William was put off by Jackie's insistence on being the boss of every aspect of their date, even though it had been he who had asked Jackie out in the first place.

William liked Jackie and wanted to take her out, and what Jackie should have done was *let him take her out*. She should have gone to the restaurant he suggested at the time he suggested, and she should have let him order the bottle of wine that he wanted to order. Jackie should have just let William be the man, and she should have just shut up and enjoyed the date!

It's not that Jackie shouldn't have opinions or that she needs to be a silent partner, but she certainly should have relinquished control of the details for the date to the man who had asked her out on the date in the first place.

When you try to control every aspect of a date, you're sending the message that you don't respect the guy or trust his decisions.

In Jackie's case, it wasn't just a message she was sending; it was the truth! Jackie didn't trust William's judgment; she didn't even trust William's restaurant suggestion when an internet search backed it up. And it had nothing to do with William; she just valued her opinion and judgment more than anyone else's.

Being bossy also sends the message that you don't think the other person is smart enough or capable enough to make the right decision. And, who wants to date that bitch?

A powerful, accomplished man wants a woman who isn't constantly trying to micro-manage his life. He wants a woman who is sexy and easy going. If you are the type of woman that needs to carry your man's balls in your purse, then there are two options for you.

The first option is that you need to find a guy who's willing to be bossed around by a woman. You want to wear the pants anyway, don't you? So go ahead; wear them. Find a guy who doesn't care what restaurant you go to and who doesn't know how to choose a great bottle of wine. He'll let you make all the decisions, and you will be in hog heaven!

Remember, though, with that comes the fact that he probably won't be as smart as you or as cultured, and he probably also won't have the money to pay for your preferred lifestyle. So, it's ALL on you, baby!

Does the thought of a man who will roll over and take whatever you throw at him turn you off? Well, that's the predicament, isn't it? You can't be the *man* and expect to be with a man.

So here is option two: tone it way down—WAY DOWN. Let those take-charge guys that you want to date know that even though you're a strong willed and very accomplished woman, you *are* willing to acquiesce, have fun, and go with the flow.

If he likes something, respect his opinion and be willing to accept it. Fight your instinct to change every plan he suggests and *just go with it*. You might be surprised to find that his favorite restaurant isn't bad at all, and instead, it's rather wonderful. Maybe that movie that he wants to see, but you have no interest in, will end up being something new and exciting, and you'll actually like it. New people and experiences open your eyes to new things. And even if you don't like it, who cares? It's just a movie, a restaurant, or a bottle of wine? Seriously, is your preferred decision more important than having a relationship with a great guy?

Meanwhile, when you feel yourself going to change a minor detail, such as changing the time of a date by a half hour, the way that Jackie did, think twice. Think about the level of importance of what you're about to change, and ask yourself, *Is this detail really so life changing that it's worth taking away the guy's power?* Because that what you're doing: you're turning your man into your little boy. Avoid it at all costs.

Plus, being in control all the time can be stressful; can it not? Always putting it on yourself to make the plans, find the restaurants, pick the movie is tiring. If you let go of some of that control that you've been so hell bent on hoarding, you might find that dating really doesn't need to be a source of stress or anxiety at all. You don't always need to be on hand with a good wine suggestion. Let the man be the man. Let him handle the details, and just go along for the ride. When you do, you'll feel a weight slip off of your shoulders, and you'll also show him that you don't mind being his woman and following his lead.

CHAPTER 5:
Dumb Bitch

When you see *this* girl coming towards you, cross the street quickly and don't make eye contact. You DON'T want to catch what she has. She could have a severe case of DBS: Dumb Bitch Syndrome.

Oh, no! Is it possible that you might already have a case DBS? Don't panic. First, let's see.

❖ DBS Alert—Take the TEST!

Occasional, mild to moderate symptoms may include the following:

- Ignoring major red flags at the start of a relationship, just because he's very cute or because you *really* want a boyfriend
- Ditching your friends (even at the last minute) because your guy calls
- Putting up with someone who has no respect for you

- Pursuing a guy who isn't pursuing you

Yikes! You do have occasional mild to moderate symptoms? Again, stay calm.

More frequent and severe symptoms may result if you continue to be with someone in spite of the following:

- The guy you're with is jobless (and has been most of his life).
- The guy has drug or alcohol problems.
- The guy you're with is a narcissist.
- Everyone (including him) says he's an asshole.
- The guy you're with is homeless. (FYI: Living with a friend or relative still means he's homeless.)
- The guy you're with doesn't support his kids if he has them.
- The guy you're with trashes his ex constantly.
- He's a player, and you know it.

The Results:

Do you know that guy? You have mild DBS.

Are you actively pursuing a relationship with that guy? You have moderate to severe DBS.

Are you sleeping with that guy? You have severe DBS.

Did any of those statements apply to your guy? A few? I know, I know: *"Oh... but he's so cute and charming, and the sex is GREAT!"* No! Don't be fooled! Losers tend to be the most charming, charismatic guys in the room. Why? Because that is the only thing they have going for them, and they have perfected those skills on many, many women before you, honey. The trouble is, they have no morals or real substance, so they'll leave you for the next opportunity as fast as they can talk you into bed—which by the way this is going, I'm thinking is pretty fast.

But wait! There are a few more symptoms we need to go over before we know for sure whether you're a lost cause or just a girl with a temporary bout of DBS.

Seek treatment right away if you *repeatedly* make these Dumb Bitch mistakes:

- You think you're in a relationship after just one or two dates.
- You jump in the sack after the first date.
- You hang on to the hope he'll call, even though he dumped you.
- Or worse, you hang on to the hope he'll call after he cheated on you AND dumped you.
- You allow a guy to treat you like an afterthought.
- You're dating or have dated a guy who was married or had a girlfriend WHILE HE WAS DATING YOU.
- You're sleeping with a guy who won't commit.
- You're always the one calling or texting him.
- You're the one always trying to see him.
- You pay for everything.

It's true, isn't it? A majority of those mistakes apply to you. It's okay. Take a deep breath. Don't worry. You are not alone. We have all been there and done that at one time or another. But, let's get you some help and fast. If this DBS takes full effect over you and you continue on this path, it could become a permanent syndrome.

✠ __Carol__

Once upon a time, Carol was a sweet, pretty, incredibly intelligent girl. She had a great deal of focus in her career and had climbed to the top of the ladder quickly. She was a supportive friend, a loyal daughter, and a caring sister. Carol was the girl that everyone wanted to be—once upon a time. However, that was before she started seeing Keith.

Keith was, for all intents and purposes, a loser, and just about everyone in town, including Carol's friends (and they thought, Carol), knew it. He had never really held a job, and because of that, he was in a huge child support dispute with his ex-wife. She was threatening to take away his right to see his children every other weekend if he didn't pay up, and the scuttlebutt in town was that he wasn't doing so. Plus, everyone knew that the reason his ex-wife had left him in the first place was that he had cheated on her with the hot (and consistently scantily clad) bartender at the dive bar downtown.

All of these reasons were why Carol's friends were *shocked* when Carol told them she had run into Keith at the grocery store and thought he was hot. Her friends were even more shocked when Carol said she was going out with Keith that night. They were even still more shocked when Carol and Keith went out quite a few times, then more times, and then more... Soon, Carol was telling her friends she thought she might actually be developing real feelings for Keith— and he had told her that he had real feelings for her.

Carol's friends exchanged confused and appalled glances before launching into their apprehensions. Lisa took the lead: "Carol, you know he's no good. You're so much better than him! He cheats on his wife, and then doesn't support his kids? What kind of a man is that? Look at you! You're accomplished. You're beautiful. You want a *family*. Why are you wasting time with a guy who couldn't even behave within the family he had?"

Carol immediately got defensive, and told her friends they were being judgmental and listening to gossip over her word. "Keith is different than he was then.

People change, you know." And besides, Carol knew she could help him with a lot of his troubles. Nobody listened to Keith, but people trusted Carol.

From there, Carol distanced herself from her friends, whom she believed were just jealous of her relationship. She ended up spending more and more time with Keith. As she did, she began to get wrapped up in all of his drama. She'd go with him to pick up his kids. She'd get in fights with his ex over the timings of their visitations, and she even appeared in court to defend Keith's position on not paying child support.

Carol became really serious about all of Keith's issues, and between that and her own job, she was really starting to change as a person. Meanwhile, old Keith reared his ugly head and his wandering eye travelled over to the scantily clad bartender in town.

While out one night, Carol saw Keith coming out of "that bar." Carol confronted Keith right there on the street and they had a huge, ugly fight that several of Carol's acquaintances witnessed, including her former friend, Lisa.

Keith swore up and down there was nothing going on between him and the bartender, but Carol's suspicions grew the more time that he spent away from her.

Eventually, she had sunken so low that one night she hid around the corner from the bar until she saw him leave at 1 a.m., and her suspicions were confirmed. He was once again with his go-to side piece: the hot bartender. Carol's heart felt like it had been ripped from her chest. She just sat in her car, sobbing and asking herself, "Why? Why? Why?!"

Why? Because a leopard doesn't change his spots just because you want him to. Just like a rattlesnake will always be a rattlesnake. These are the laws of nature, and a cheating loser will always be a cheating loser.

His View

"Carol was great at first, but I meet great women all the time. The ladies love me. Thinking about her now, though, just turns me off. She got so serious and controlling and involved in my life, and following me to the bar? Geez, how pathetic. All I know is that Carol went from being exciting and fun to being serious and insane. Yeah, I went out with that bartender again. So what? What else was I supposed to do? She's sexy and exciting, and that's what I want. This is who I am, and Carol knew that all along."

The Reality

From the moment Carol got involved with Keith, all she could see was his good looks and his charm. When she was put in the position of defending him, she did it gladly. Carol was trying to rescue Keith, and she was trying to fix him, simply because she liked his outside.

A lot of things can contribute to a smart girl making dumb choices, but the biggest factor is getting stuck in that fantasy of "I can change him. He needs me to help him, and then he'll be perfect." The truth is, though, if he wasn't perfect to begin with, he never will be.

Stories like that are all around us--in books, in magazines, in movies, etc. The sweet girl turns the bad boy soft, and he becomes Prince Charming. A frog is transformed into a prince. Those stories are invented, though. In reality, people don't change from one thing to another.

Sometimes they get wrapped up in something—like Carol did with Keith's drama—but they don't change at their core. Keith wasn't going to either. In fact, if anyone changed, it was Carol—and not for the better. Once you sink into the trenches and you think you're "in love," it's hard to climb out.

A lack of self-respect, a desire to "fix" bad boys, and a major bout of fantasy thinking are present in smart women who fall prey to being dumb at different times in their life. For a lot of girls, attention from a "bad boy"—someone who your friends and family think isn't your "type"—can give you an injection of excitement and rebellion or even empowerment.

Be careful, though. The reality is that it isn't what you think it is at all. It's a high, and it's fuelled by your desire to feel special. Involvement with guys like this are like a drug, and like a drug, they're addictive, destructive, and turn you into someone you're not: a Dumb Bitch.

If you have DBS, we probably don't need to focus on how to get you a boyfriend. You'll find plenty of losers who are willing to emotionally abuse you and take advantage of your fantasy thinking. No, what we need to do is remind you that love shouldn't be a series of highs and lows. *Love shouldn't hurt;* love should feel good. If it doesn't feel good, then it isn't love.

Do you remember who you were before him? Do you remember that strong-willed, smart, and sassy girl? Is that who he's with right now? Or is he with a girl who is making stupid decisions and is essentially putting herself on track to be in an unfulfilling relationship, where in the end, she's going to get burned?

If what you ultimately want is a long-term, happy, healthy relationship, stop trying to fix the bad boys. Stop trying to turn a frog into a prince. He's a frog for goodness sakes, and he ALWAYS will be.

What you need to do is to remember who you were before—who you are deep down inside. You are a confident and beautiful woman, deserving of a guy who loves and respects you. You deserve someone who is your equal—someone who can improve and add to the quality of your life, not the other way around.

CHAPTER 6:

Freaky Bitch

Step right up! Step right up! Behold the powers of... the magical vagina! That's right, girls! Your lady parts have special fairy dust within them that (POOF!) turns strangers into boyfriends with just one visit! So go ahead, drop your panties! Jump in the sack! It's time to convert that date of yours into the partner you've been longing for!

Hmm... sound a little too good to be true? That's because *it is* too good to be true.

Time for the harsh, sad reality! Ready? Vaginas aren't enchanted—at all, not even a little bit. They cannot, do not, and WILL NOT convert a first date into a lifelong relationship. The only thing that sleeping with him too fast is going to turn him into is a "one night stand" or a "fling." That's not exactly what you're after, huh?

❖ <u>**Freaky Alert—Take the TEST!**</u>

You might be a Freaky Bitch if:

- Your idea of getting to know him involves his genitals.

And, that's all! Did you pass or fail?

Freaky bitches aren't future wife material, and they don't get boyfriends. Don't get me wrong; guys *really* enjoy spending time (having sex) with them.   But, that's about it.

I know what you're thinking.   *So what if I sleep around? Guys do it all the time. They'll sleep with a girl on the first date. Why can't I do the same? I can have sex just like a guy—no strings attached. I'm just having fun. I'm an independent woman!* That's all true and power to the ladies, but let's take a second to remember that if you're reading this book, then you obviously want a boyfriend. If you wanted to run around sleeping with whomever you want with no strings attached, you wouldn't be reading this; would you? What you want is to be someone's girlfriend and,

I'm sure, eventually, someone's wife. And the thing is that even though you're telling yourself (and probably the guy) that you don't want a relationship, you and I know that that is just bullshit. While, I'm sure you're saying that you can do it like a guy because you're a free, independent woman, there is also little voice inside of you that's saying something else. I promise you that voice is saying:

"I'm so good in bed, so hot, so crazy, that he won't be able to resist me. He's going to have one taste and be addicted. He's going to need me, and he's going to stay with me. He will want to see me all the time, and then, what was a one-night fling is going to become a many-nights fling. Eventually..."

Eventually...? Eventually what? *"And eventually I'll be his girlfriend."* Do you really believe that your vagina can cast a spell over him that will make him see you as anything other than a one-night stand?

Girl, let's be honest; you're trying to turn him into your boyfriend using the wrong bait! Class and restraint are better ingredients for a magic potion.

�֎ <u>Sarah</u>

Sarah had always had a crush on her friend Blake. Unfortunately, he was married, so it wasn't meant to be. But one day, while out with mutual friends that Sarah and Blake shared, Sarah was shocked (and kind of happy) to hear that Blake's wife Mindy had left him for her trainer! Their friends went on to say that Blake was totally devastated and that they were all taking him out to dinner that weekend to try to cheer him up. They invited Sarah, and Sarah said she'd definitely be there.

Sarah felt badly for Blake, but that didn't stop her from thinking that perhaps now it was her chance with Blake. So, although she wanted to be there for him as a friend, she also saw this as a chance to "wow" him. Sarah showed up to dinner looking her absolute hottest and sexiest, and she made sure to get the seat at the table right next to Blake.

Sarah listened sympathetically as Blake poured his heart out to the group about the breakup and how hard it had been on him. His wife had only left a week prior, and the wounds here still very fresh. When each friend reminded Blake that they were there for him, Sarah echoed their words, and she even rubbed Blake's back sympathetically. As everyone was leaving the restaurant, Sarah asked Blake if he'd like to go to the bar down the street for a little nightcap to continue to talk. He graciously declined, saying he was just so worn out from everything that had been going on. Sarah said no problem, and she offered to cook him dinner sometime. It was clear to their entire group of friends, though, that Sarah had set her sights on Blake far beyond a home cooked meal.

Anxious to get their date set, Sarah called Blake several times to follow up on her offer to make him dinner, but Blake always said he was busy. About a month later, Sarah was at a local sports bar with some friends when she spied Blake across the room. Sarah excused herself to the bathroom, reapplied her lipstick, made sure she looked as hot as possible. Then, she blazed a trail across the bar to Blake. It was apparent to Sarah right away that Blake had been drinking for awhile, so she flirted with him mercilessly until eventually, Blake couldn't resist Sarah's temptations anymore. They kissed. After the kiss, Sarah convinced Blake that he should really let her make him dinner the following night, and Blake agreed.

When Blake showed up for dinner, Sarah was looking super hot, and the dinner was rather romantic. Sarah made pasta, got a great bottle of wine, and lit candles on the table. Blake thanked Sarah for the dinner and said that it was all really nice, but that he wanted to make sure that Sarah understood that he wasn't ready for a relationship right now. Sarah put her hand on Blake's knee and smiled. She said, "Of course. Me neither. I'm just enjoying your company. Just because you don't want to have a relationship doesn't mean you can't have fun, right?" With that, Sarah leaned over, kissed Blake, and placed her hand in his lap. She made sure to be extra crazy in bed, knowing that she was putting on a much better show than Blake's conservative wife ever had. Blake concurred; they had a *great* time together. They went out two more times that same week, and both times, the night ended the same way: crazy, wild sex.

After their third encounter though, Sarah didn't hear from Blake for a couple of days. She was a bit distraught, and so she sent him text after text. His responses were fairly short and uninspired.

Sarah was devastated. She was sure that after Blake had such a good time with her that she had changed his mind about having a relationship. I mean, after all, he slept with her three times.

Eventually, she had to confide in a mutual friend about how hurt she was, because the group was going out. Since Sarah knew Blake would be there, she just felt too strange joining in.

His View

"I told Sarah I didn't want a relationship, and she said she didn't either. I don't get why she would have lied about that. I mean, at first I did think she had feelings for me, which is why I kept ignoring her dinner invitations. I had a talk with her where I explained that I really wasn't ready for a relationship. I *just* broke up with my wife! I'm not ready to be in another relationship. I thought Sarah knew that. I feel bad I hurt her, but I felt like I was upfront and honest. I figured she was being honest too when she said she just wanted to have fun."

The Reality

Blake was a good guy. He was upfront and honest with Sarah. Sarah, however, wasn't upfront OR honest with Blake. No one deserves a bait and switch, especially poor Blake. Sarah was left feeling like she was "done wrong" by Blake, but seriously, she only had herself to blame. She could have avoided her hurt feelings had she listened to Blake and really heard what he was saying. Instead, Sarah discounted what Blake was saying. She knew she had feelings for him, and because of that, her goal was to transform him from friend to boyfriend. Sarah believed that sex was going to do that; she thought those *magical powers* were going to change Blake's mind about having a relationship.

Although Sarah had known Blake for a while through friends, women do this all the time with guys they've just met. They strip off their clothes and jump into bed way too quickly, assuming that doing so will allow them to bypass the normal "getting to know you" phase of dating and will take them straight from point A (meeting) to point B (relationship). It won't.

When you go on dates, you size people up. There's nothing wrong with that; it's just what you have to do. You need to evaluate, based on the signals you get, what kind of person you're out with. Based on that evaluation, you decide what kind of guy you think your date is and whether or not he'd make a good partner—a good boyfriend, husband, and even a good father. We do this both consciously and unconsciously in big and small ways. And based on those evaluations, we decide if we want to see the guy again.

It should come as no surprise that guys do this too. And by and large, the girls that men date usually fall into one of three categories:

1. "I would never do her."
2. "I'd only do her."
3. "She's relationship material."

What's actually at work here is not categories but very different types of chemistry and, therefore, very different types of relationships.

Sexual (short-term) relationships start out with a bang (literally), but they end with hurt feelings, usually yours, pretty quickly. Why? There's no substance. To put it in terms of literal chemistry, the sexual relationship forms in a quick reaction. Man and woman mix, and (POOF!) there's a lot of sex and a lot of kink, but there is nothing much else. The smoke from a quick reaction clears rather rapidly, and then, judgment and doubt sets in.

"She slept with me right away. Does she do that with everyone? Where did she learn those moves? Only with LOTS of practice!"

Long-term relationships, on the other hand, start with a clean slate, move slowly, and are an investment of building substance. Emotional connection, having things in common, great conversation, friendship—it's all mixed together. Things heat up and heat up and heat up, until finally, all that substance is boiling over.

You've got yourself an intense, sexy, whirlwind, full-of-butterflies relationship.

What Sarah was projecting—the signal she was sending and verbally saying—was that she just wanted to have a good time, no strings attached. Men are literal; what they say is what they mean. That's it. Stop trying to make more of it. They hear what you say and take it the way they mean it, literally. So obviously, Blake thought they were having just what they both said they were going to have: a good time. He wasn't looking for anyone to put in the "long-term relationship" category, so of course, he put her in the "good time girl" category. Ingredients were mixed quickly, and (POOF!) it got hot and wild right away. Two people with two different intentions: a recipe for disaster.

If you're being thrown into the "fun" category right away, the chances are very slim that a guy is also looking at you as a potential long-term partner. You'll know it by how quick he is to push you into the bedroom. Guys usually only try to have sex with a girl right away if they don't really like her for the long term. So when a girl comes along that he has a real connection with, how much do you want to bet he'll drop the girls in the "fun" category to spend more time with "the long-term potential?" After all, the slow budding romance is what most of us are after. Girls in the fun category are seat fillers; they keep a guy pleased until a "potential wife" comes along to take the seat. It may not be a pretty truth, but it's the truth. Freaky bitches don't get boyfriends. They get freaky, and they get left behind.

So how do you get in that "long-term" category, if that's what you want? Well, first of all, be a *lady (not a bitch)* for as long as you can. Guys want a girl who respects herself, who puts herself on a pedestal. You have standards; you don't just give it up. Wait until the time is right, until the ingredients have mixed and heated up. If he really likes you, then he will be willing to become your boyfriend *before* you have sex.

Don't project something you're not. You want a boyfriend; you want someone you can get to know and spend time with. Most importantly, *you want someone who wants to take the time to get to know you.* Don't tell yourself or him anything different.

Sex can be great and fun, but it's not a way to convert a date into a boyfriend!

CHAPTER 7:
Frumpy Bitch

Oh! I must have caught you on your way to the grocery store or the gym, huh? No? Oh. I just figured since you're wearing those unflattering pants and you're hardly wearing any makeup, you must be headed...Oh, wait a minute. What are you saying? A date? No, no. NO! You're not wearing THAT on a date, are you?

Sexless Sally just showed up for a date with Hot Hank. I wonder how this will play out...

❖ **Frumpy Alert—Take the TEST!**

Is it possible that YOU aren't putting enough effort into your appearance for dates? If so, you might be a Frumpy Bitch! Have you ever:

- Worn flats on a date?
- Pulled your hair back in a ponytail for a date rather than doing your hair?
- Preferred to be "comfortable" rather than "sexy?"

- Worn the same clothes on your date that you wore to work?
- Worn your mom jeans on a date?
- Threw on that "5 years ago dress" and headed out the door?
- Not put on fresh makeup for a date? ("Freshening up" doesn't count. I mean FRESH makeup.)
- Thought, "I want to be loved and appreciated for *who I am*," and therefore, you show up as plain Jane rather than Tarzan meets Jane?

What do you think? Guilty as charged? Are you a Frumpy Bitch in need of some TLC? **T**ough **L**essons in **C**lothing?

Ladies, I'm going to tell you something that I have heard from many, many men that is perhaps a nasty little truth, but it's a truth nonetheless: when you show up to a date, especially a blind date or just a first date, the guy you're meeting will determine in the first thirty seconds of meeting you whether or not he's attracted to you. That's it. Those thirty seconds are your *very small* window of time to "wow" him. When the guy sees you, he needs to think, *Yep, I'd do her!* If he doesn't think that, you won't be going on a second date.

I know. I know. *Relationships are not just about sex,* but attraction is one of the key ingredients. Deciding to date someone is undeniably about sexual attraction, especially with men; that attraction starts (or ends) the first moment they lay eyes on you. Sure, eventually he will care if you're smart or interesting, but at this point, we're focusing on the all-important initial reaction. The thing that makes him sit up and take notice, that spark of electricity that happens because YOU ARE HOT! No spark? No chemistry. No chemistry? No second date. No second date? No boyfriend!

�֎ Sandra

Sandra was just like many other single women her age. She had a good job, some great friends, but no boyfriend. She was getting to an age where she needed to start thinking about having a family. So, she did what most busy working professionals do these days; she started online dating and told her friends and family that if they knew of anyone they wanted to set her up with, she was open and willing to go on dates.

Through online dating and friends, Sandra was set up on quite a few dates. However, she had a very no-nonsense approach to dating. Sandra was an accomplished professional woman, after all, and she wasn't looking for someone who was superficial. She wanted a man who was smart, preferably an Ivy League guy, who liked her for who she was and who would essentially make a good long-term partner and a great father to children. She wanted someone cute, like everyone does, but above all, his intellect was her number one criteria.

Because Sandra put all of her emphasis on education, accomplishments, and intellect, she rarely dressed much different for dates then she would for work or going to dinner with friends. At least for work, she had a "professional business suit look" and had to put some effort into that. But, when it came to dating, she just wanted to be "herself."

As her day-to-day wardrobe of choice, she preferred comfy jeans, cozy oversized sweaters, and ballet slippers. So, unfortunately they became elements of her dating wardrobe. Sandra's dates had two choices: weekend comfy or just-got-out-of-work frumpy. When she'd set dates for after work, she wouldn't even bother to go home to change or put on fresh makeup, she'd just head out and go straight there. And if the date was set for a weekend, he'd get to meet casual Sandra, in her comfy clothes. There was no such thing as sexy Sandra.

Sandra started to notice a pattern in the men she was meeting for dates. Regardless of whether they had found each other online or were set up through a friend, many of the dates Sandra went on were very polite and very nice, but they never seemed overly excited to be meeting her. And even though she thought they had great conversations, none of the men Sandra saw were asking her on second dates. Sandra, who knew she was a great girl with a lot to offer, just couldn't figure out what the problem was.

His View

Let's see what a couple of the guys Sandra went on dates with had to say:

Peter: "On Sandra's online profile, she had a picture of herself where she was all dressed up and looked great. I don't know, but she must have been at a wedding or some other special event. Anyway, she showed up to the date, and she looked like she was just running to the grocery store to pick up some milk or her dry cleaning. She didn't do her hair; she wore very little makeup; and although her clothes looked like they were from J Crew, I'm not interested in dating someone who looks like my sister. Sure, she was smart and educated, but I just wasn't that attracted to her—and that's a big part of it for me."

Dan: "Sandra seemed like a really nice person, but she had no sex appeal. And actually, she seems like she could be sexy, if she put some effort in, but, it didn't seem like being sexy was important to her. At the end of the day, I have to want to defile my woman, even if she is a Harvard graduate."

The Reality

You MUST "bring it" if you are going on a date. What does "bring it" mean? It means bring your A-Game. If you have a guy that wants to meet you and he wants to take you out, get your ass all fixed up, walk in, and blow him away! That's what "bring it" means!

So, we all know what I'm going to say here: Sandra was NOT bringing it! Somewhere in her decision to seek smart men, she forgot that appearances MATTER. When you phone it in and don't put any effort into your appearance for a date, you're sending one of two messages:

1) "I don't care what you think of me."
2) "This is the best I can do."

Neither one is true, and neither one is going to get you a second date!

When you go on dates, you need to "sex it up" (not slut it up) and be attractive. To be attractive, you have to be sexy and feminine. Baggy pants, casual shirts, and flats are not sexy or feminine; they're frumpy. Come on, girl! Pamper yourself a little. Go to that cute boutique in your neighborhood and buy several outfits that are NOT what you'd wear with the girls. A little black dress or a sexy top and skirt will go a long way. Buy yourself something feminine and flirty that shows off your figure and highlights your best assets. You want him to know that you dressed for *him*. Show up for a date looking like you're dressed to be social and fun, while also feeling like yourself. You want your "date clothes" to be outfits that you would feel overdressed doing your grocery shopping in and that you could NEVER wear to work, but not something so over the top that it could never be you. Now, I'm not saying dress slutty; no, just dress sexy, feminine, and flirty. Don't show *too much skin*. A little cleavage is fine, but don't give him too much of a show, just yet...

Now, do we all need to look like supermodels in magazines? No, we don't. Among women and men, there is a wide range of beauty, and there are many different qualities we are all attracted to. So, no, you don't have to look like Gisele Bündchen to look HOT. But, you do need to look like the supermodel version of *you.* And I know you know what that means: **be the best you can be.**

Before your next date, go down this checklist to prepare yourself. I guarantee you will not only look *amazing*, you'll feel amazing too!

- ✓ **Pick out an outfit *specifically for your date.***
  Wear something flattering and sexy, but don't show too much skin. A fitted little black dress will do the trick every time.
- ✓ **Wear some sexy lingerie.**
  Don't let him see it, but knowing it's there will make you feel sexy and powerful!
- ✓ **You should absolutely wear heels**.
  Heels make your legs look much sexier, trust me. Sexy, strappy heels are a must-add—the higher, the better.
- ✓ **Do your hair!**
  Avoid simply pulling your hair back in a ponytail, and for goodness sakes, do NOT wear your hear in a messy bun! Use hair products; turn on a hair straightener or a curling iron; and style your hair in

the most flattering way. Even better, go to the salon and get blow out!

✓ **Pop in your contacts, and leave the glasses at home.**

You might think they're quirky or make you look smart, but trust me: contacts show off your eyes and are definitely the way to go. Glasses have a time and place (feel free to wear them at home when you're alone), but their place is NOT on dates! And if you only need glasses for driving, then leave them in the car.

✓ **Tweeze or wax your eyebrows, and play up your eyes.**

Don't under estimate the power of long, lush lashes. Let your eyes do the talking!

✓ **Put on a fresh coat of makeup.**

Don't just "freshen up" your work face. Wash your face, and start all over. A new date is a new day, and a new day deserves its own face.

✓ **Always have a fresh manicure and pedicure.**

✓ **Accessorize your outfit with jewelry.**

✓ **Wear perfume, or a scented lotion.**

Wear a scent that makes you feel good and smell good!

✓ **Check yourself out in the mirror and see how HOT you look!**

That is called bringing your A-Game! And your appearance isn't the only thing that will change by bringing it. You won't believe how good you will feel when you spend time pampering yourself. You'll look sexy; you'll feel sexy; and you'll act sexy. Trust me! Now go out and get yourself some sexy date clothes and some naughty new lingerie. While you're at it, get your hair done and buy yourself some new makeup. You're out to meet men and your future husband, so *dress accordingly.*

One last but important thing to mention: if you are using online dating sites, you need to show accurate photos. Three recent, RECENT photos are fine—one that looks your VERY best, one that looks like regular you, and one body shot. Don't use a bathing suit photo; otherwise, you will give him the wrong idea. Keep in mind that you never want to show up and have the guy squint and cock his head to the side trying to recognize you.

You *always* want to show up to that first meeting and have him to say, "Wow! You're even prettier than your picture!" Enhance your best qualities, and whatever you do, make sure you look *your* very best when you walk in the room. Guys are visual, so give him something to look at and enjoy.

And by the way, who cares if you don't end up liking him? It's all about you looking *your* best so that you can have as many options as *you* need or want to have!

CHAPTER 8:
Insecure Bitch

Coming soon to a theatre near you...

A horror story of epic proportions! When a beautiful girl with winning qualities is bitten by a mutant bug, it plants a parasite in her brain. This particularly terrifying parasite eats away at the brain of the poor unsuspecting girl, and worse: the only way to keep the parasite from eating her alive is to feed it compliments and validation from poor, unfortunate, unsuspecting humans.

The infected girl tries as hard as she can to avoid feeding on her friends and boyfriend, but before long, the parasite (more commonly known as insecurity) is growing and growing and GROWING! And as the insecurity grows, it gets HUNGRIER! The once wonderful girl is quickly transformed into a practically *unrecognizable creature! BEWARE!* **It's the Insecure Bitch!** *She's running loose, and she's taking her friends and boyfriend hostage! She's feeding on their compliments and validation, and it won't be long before she's hungry for more! Her victims, meanwhile, are running scared!*

YIKES! Unfortunately, for many girls, this is more than just a movie—it's real life. Could this crazed creature be you?

❖ <u>Insecure Alert—Take the TEST!</u>

Answer the following questions to see if this might just be you:

- Are you afraid to show off your body for fear that you look fat?
- Are you afraid to show off your body for fear that you look too thin?
- Are you starting to get too much botox?
- Do you constantly think of ways that you could improve your appearance?

- Are you afraid to voice your opinion because you think you're not smart enough?
- Do you compare yourself to other girls constantly?
- When a man gives you a compliment, do you think, "That's not true?"
- Or worse, do you SAY, "That's not true?"
- Are you threatened by other women?
- Do you get jealous of every girl who steps within ten feet of a guy you're dating, because you're sure she's prettier than you and that he'd rather be with her?

So, has the creature reared its ugly head in your life? Are you a secure, confident woman? Or an Insecure Bitch? Well, I think you're great, and I just need you to know it! Help is on the way!

✳ Meghan

Meghan was amidst a major life change. About two years ago, she got serious about her health. She went on a diet, and she started working out. She had recently made her weight loss goal of losing thirty pounds, and she felt really accomplished because of it. Before she decided to get in shape, Meghan had felt really bad about her self-image. She knew she was overweight, and she knew she could be healthier. So just before she decided to make the major change in her life, Meghan had all but stopped dating. She was too inhibited by her perception of herself. While she was focusing on her health, she put dating totally on the backburner. Now that she had made her weight loss goal and was feeling healthier, and sexier, she made an online dating profile and also started to let her friends set her up on some dates.

Meghan went out on several dates, but she never really hit it off with anyone—until she met Jason. Finally, her love life was in full swing. They really got along and had great chemistry. Jason had been in a long-term relationship previously, and, like Meghan, he had taken some time off from the dating scene while he figured things out for himself. Now, he was ready for a new long-term relationship, and he made sure to find someone different from his last girlfriend.

Since he and Meghan really hit it off, they started seeing each other a lot. Quickly, they became exclusive.

For the first couple of weeks that Meghan was with Jason, she was elated. He was so different from guys she had dated in the past, and he made her really happy. She had fun when she was with him, and she thought of him often when they were apart. She was really starting to fall for him.

Everything was going well until one night, when Meghan was at Jason's apartment, she was using his computer and stumbled across a picture of him with a rail thin, extremely beautiful girl.

"Who's this?" Meghan asked, while thinking, *Please say your sister, or someone else. Just please don't say—*

"Oh, that's my ex-girlfriend," Jason answered. And once he said it, it was as if a ghost from Meghan's past moved into in her head and absolutely refused to leave. Meghan's old insecurities of herself and her image came flooding back into her mind, and suddenly, she doubted the success she'd had in losing her weight.

Sure, I weigh less than I used to, but I'm still not model skinny. And I'll never be as pretty as that girl. Why do I even bother?

Meghan's focus on this and her descent into self-doubt started to cause great deals of worry and stress within her. When Meghan was with Jason, her anxiety drove her to ask him really leading and awkward questions. She would ask him if he thought she was pretty or if he liked what she was wearing. Even though Meghan was clearly fishing for complements, Jason would always give them to her. He truly did think Meghan was beautiful, so it wasn't hard for him to play into her hand. But, no matter how many times Jason complemented Meghan, she wasn't hearing him. She still thought, *But I'm not as pretty as your last girlfriend.*

This thought haunted Meghan, and finally, one day, she let it slip out. "Do you wish you were still with your ex-girlfriend instead of me?"

Her question took Jason aback, and he said, "What do you mean?"

Megan looked around sheepishly before saying, "Well, I mean, do you like me as much as you liked her? More? I'm not as pretty as her. Do you wish you were with her still?"

Jason leaned in, kissed Meghan, and told her that it didn't matter how pretty any girl in the entire world was, Meghan was the prettiest girl and the only girl he wanted to be with.

Meghan smiled and tried to believe him, but deep down, Meghan's insecurity was at work, turning her into someone who depended on constant validation from Jason. She became constantly focused on—and in a large sense, defined herself by—how pretty or thin Jason thought she was.

With Meghan constantly doubting their relationship, Jason began to feel like he couldn't do anything right. No matter how hard he tried to prove to Meghan that he cared about her and thought the world of her, she didn't believe him. Soon, Meghan was always thinking about her self-perceived inadequacies; she was literally driving herself crazy.

One day, while left alone with Jason's phone, Meghan picked it up and started gazing through his text messages, emails, and recent calls, checking to see if he had secretly been corresponding with his ex. He hadn't, but that didn't ease Meghan's suspicions. She was convinced Jason still carried a flame for his ex and checked his phone every time she was left alone with it.

Meghan never found anything on Jason's phone, but Jason found Meghan—red-handed. With his phone in her hand, she didn't know what to do other than tell him the truth. She told him that she was checking up on him. For Jason, this was the final straw. Hurt and upset, Jason ended things with Meghan. There was no winning with her, and Jason just couldn't fight the losing battle anymore.

His View

"I was really falling for Meghan—big time. We were both kind of at the same place in life, and we both were hoping for someone who we could spend time with long-term. When I met Meghan, I was excited, because frankly, she was everything my ex was not.

"First of all, yes, my ex girlfriend was a model, and that was the problem. She was constantly preoccupied with perfection. Having to constantly reassure her how beautiful she was and how great she was didn't make for a fun, balanced, or even normal relationship.

"So, when I met Meghan, I was thrilled. She wasn't a model. She wasn't beauty queen, but she was beautiful to me. She seemed like a normal girl, and that's what I wanted. I wanted someone who liked herself as much as I liked her. And Meghan really seemed like she was that girl!

"The problems started when Meghan could not get over the fact that I had a girlfriend who was a model, and she was always comparing herself to my ex, which was crazy, because she never even met my ex. Plus, my ex was the opposite of my ideal girl!

"I thought Meghan was secure and strong, and that's what attracted me to her. But, in the end, Meghan was just as insecure as my old girlfriend. And after spending two years of constantly trying to convince someone that they were beautiful, that they were great, and that they were perfect, I was exhausted. I had told myself I would never go through that again."

The Reality

Insecurity did to Meghan what it does to most girls: it made her anxious. She didn't trust in her own worth. Meghan also didn't trust that there was truth in what Jason was telling her about his feelings towards her. Meghan doubted Jason's intentions, even though he gave her no reason to, and that caused her to self-destruct within the relationship.

A lot of times, insecurities are fed by previous experiences, the same way Meghan's were. She was constantly thinking about what she used to look like and how she used to feel, and she began projecting those problems onto her new relationship. For some people, insecurity comes from something that happened to them as kids. A teacher told you that you weren't very smart once, and ever since, you've been subconsciously seeking validation that you're intelligent. A parent or sibling told you that you weren't pretty or even simply didn't tell you how pretty you were often enough, so now you stay afloat on compliments from others.

Sometimes, you may not even realize that you're seeking it, but when you have deep-rooted insecurities, your livelihood depends on validation. For many, many girls, the perceived solution to the emptiness left behind by the lack of that validation is finding a man who provides constant consolation against their insecurities.

If your man tells you that you are pretty every day, you are able to believe it's true. However, because that self-worth isn't coming from within, it's temporary. It wears off. Before long, you're seeking validation again.

As Jason points out, for guys especially, being put upon to be the only source of a girl's self-esteem is tiring. When a girl says, "I feel fat," her guy will, more times than not, say, "Of course you're not fat. You're beautiful and perfect." But, press him enough times for compliments, and he'll start to feel like nothing he says has any value. The truth is that he does think his girlfriend is beautiful, and he'd bend over backwards if it would help convince her. But when insecurity is at work, no matter how hard he tries, he can never silence that little voice in her head, and that voice vetoes his opinion every time. That's draining, and it makes him feel like nothing he says is ever good enough—which is absolutely not how you want to make a guy, a friend, or anyone feel! Insecurity is a very deep and powerful feeling.

Your constant need for validation is, as we've said, unfair to the man you're seeing, but it's *especially* unfair to you. If you define yourself in terms of how someone else thinks of you, then you are not your own person. Needing someone else to think you're great because you don't realize it yourself leads to making the totally wrong dating decisions—whether it's picking the wrong guy consistently or acting out in ways that are destructive to a relationship the way Meghan did.

You need to teach yourself to accept that when someone tells you that they want to spend time with you, you have to trust them enough to believe them. You need to remind yourself that insecurity exists, and that when you're thinking things like, *What if I'm not pretty enough for him?* that's insecurity. It's not logic, and especially not truth, doing the talking.

So, how do you fight insecurity? This issue can go so deep that you might require a professional's help to get through it, and there is nothing wrong with that. It is possible to win the battle, though; it just requires a lot of effort to reassure yourself that you are great and that you are the best you can be. No one is perfect, and I mean NO ONE. Besides, in my opinion, it's boring to be perfect, so just be glad you're you. And remember, men don't want perfect; they just want a woman who feels sexy and confident in her own skin—imperfections and all.

CHAPTER 9:

Irrational Bitch

And now, an excerpt from the *Best of the Bitches Cookbook, Volume 1.*

For this recipe you will need the following:

- *One guy*
- *One girl*
- *Sprinkling of passion*
- *Sprinkling of chemistry*
- *One bowl filled with of three cups of irrational drama*

Preheat oven to "hot." Once oven is heated, place guy and girl next to one another inside. Let them get nice and hot—they'll start to meld together, forming to one another a bit. This is normal. Sprinkle the mixture with passion and chemistry. Let it cook a little longer, and the guy and girl should start to get even closer, baking into one solid unit more and more as time moves forward.

Now, just as it's starting to get really fused, take the guy and girl formation out of the steamy oven and toss it into your bowl of irrational drama. Guy and girl should separate immediately and float around in the bowl together a while until eventually the bowl of irrational drama starts to eat away at them. Take them out and separate them if you'd like to salvage them at all. If not, let them soak in the irrational drama. They will eventually disintegrate.

Oops! Silly me. I forgot to tell you what that was a recipe for before you started doing it. That was a recipe for disaster!

❖ Irrational Alert—Take the TEST!

Have you ever met a guy and suddenly you feel that steaming pile of crazy in the pit of your stomach? This is one of the very first indicators that you might be an Irrational Bitch, but let's make sure.

- Do you often find yourself wrapped up in very dramatic situations?
- Do your friends tend to tell you that you are overreacting to a situation?
- Do you often seek the advice of your friends, but when they give you advice, you turn around and do the exact opposite?
- Do you make up a million different stories in your head of things that you're sure your guy is doing, but yet your ideas have no ground?
- Does the smallest thing send you into a tailspin?

Okay, we'll stop there. How many of those did you answer yes to? Even if you answered yes to one of those questions, you might just be cooking up a big bowl of irrational drama that you'll end up tossing your lovely relationship right into.

Irrational side, listen up!

Irrational women can often time start out as sane, capable women; however, the minute a man enters the equation all sense of reason goes out the window.

Suddenly, with a guy in the picture, the (once completely rational woman) becomes irrational and is incapable of standing on solid ground. This is because solid ground is made up of logical reasoning, and that is not something that an Irrational Bitch is in touch with when it comes to a relationship with a man—period.

The problem is that most guys (most people, actually) live in that logical place called reality. And, crazy, irrational B.S., like invented stories, drama, and exaggerated emotional reactions, does not generally occupy their minds.

While you're off creating chaos and hanging out on Planet Crazy, where do you think all the good guys are? That's right: Planet Reality—with all the sane girls. They might come and visit once and a while, but I promise you, you will scare them off with your crazy accusations. Quickly, they will take what they need and return as fast as they can back to Planet Reality. So, until we can get you to there too, you are going to be out there, on another planet, all ALONE.

Come on, sister! Snap out it! You need to stop it with the crazy bitch stuff, pronto!

✠ Rachael

Rachael was at the dentist one day when the guy sitting next to her in the waiting room, Chad, struck her as very cute and very charming. They started chatting and before Rachael knew it, she had given Chad her phone number. She didn't know anything about him other than that he was charming and had great teeth, but she had a good feeling about him.

Chad called her the next day to tell her it was great meeting her and that he'd love to take her out, but he was leaving in two days to visit his parents back east for a couple of weeks. So, an amazing romantic dinner date led to lunch the next day before Chad left. Rachael was so smitten that she even offered to drive Chad to the airport that night. With a long kiss goodbye at the gate, Rachel (in her mind) was already planning their wedding.

Chad seemed like a great guy. He was funny, smart, and had a great job; he was everything that Rachael was looking for in a partner. And he was very taken with her. During the two weeks that he was away, Chad called often, and they ended up always having very long conversations. A real connection between them was forming.

However, all of that was about to change very quickly. One night, a few days before Chad was to return from his trip, Rachael had just gotten home from a long, stressful day at work. She was starting to get anxious because she hadn't heard from Chad all day, and she immediately *thought* something was off. So, she decided to call Chad to see what he was up to. When she called, it went directly to voicemail. She didn't leave a message, but instead, she waited a few minutes. Then, she sent him a text that read, "Call me." A little while later, he called, and he sounded happy to be talking to Rachael. Rachael began to tell him about her day, but all that she could hear was the blaring music and a group of laughing girls in the background.

She paused. "Where are you? Who was that?" she asked.

Chad said, "Oh, I'm out with some friends." He asked her to continue her story. She did, but her enthusiasm was trailing off while thoughts of "I'm out with friends" flooded her mind.

Finally, she stopped herself and said, "Chad, who are you with? Girls?"

Chad said, "No, I'm just with some friends—"

Just as he was about to finish his sentence, his phone died. Rachael was stunned. She didn't know if he hung up on her or if a girl had hung up his phone for him. All of a sudden, Rational Rachel was gone, and in her place stood Crazy Rachael. The Irrational Bitch was unleashed.

Pacing around her kitchen not knowing what to do, she called her friend Laura and told her the story.

"Hmmmm... Yep, that sounds strange, but I'm sure he'll call you tomorrow and explain. From what you've told me so far before today, he seems like a great guy. Just give him the benefit of the doubt and wait for him to call you. "

Rachael hung up with Laura, but she just couldn't calm her mind. She slammed around her kitchen for a while before flopping down on the couch with her laptop and deciding to do some Facebook investigation. She immediately clicked on Chad's profile and went into his pictures. What Rachael saw sent her spiraling into what was essentially a fit. On Facebook, Rachael saw pictures of Chad out on the town with various people, and there were plenty of women—at bars, at restaurants, even at some of their houses. There were pictures of Chad at a family picnic where other people were holding kids, but he wasn't. At the same picnic, there were repeated pictures of Chad and one girl in particular who Rachael learned through Facebook was named Samantha.

Rachael scrolled down Chad's Facebook wall and saw that this Samantha had posted several times on Chad's wall with things like "Can't wait for this weekend!" and "I WILL beat you at pool—NEXT TIME!" Samantha and Chad were clearly all too familiar, and Rachael wasn't going to have any of it.

Steaming, Rachael then dialed her other friend Kendra. When Kendra answered, Rachael launched into her monologue. "Well, it looks like Chad isn't who I thought he was! I was on the phone with him, and I heard loud music and girls laughing talking in the background. Then, I went to his Facebook page, and the writing is (quite literally) on the wall! This girl is constantly messaging him, and there are tons of pictures of them together—even pictures of her with his family! How long do you think he's been dating her? What is he doing? Is he just stringing me along?"

Kendra was taken aback by this story, and she asked Rachael if she was sure there was something going on with Chad and this Samantha girl. Kendra even reminded Rachael that she barely knew Chad anyway because they had only gone on two dates. So she could hardly lay claim to him, anyway. Still in a fury and ignoring Kendra's voice of reality, Rachael said, "Of course, I'm sure! I saw it all with my own eyes!"

After hanging up with Kendra, Rachael once again tried to calm herself down, but she couldn't. In spite of herself, she sent Chad a text message that read: "Was it

Samantha? Is that who was there earlier?" She then immediately sent another text: "I saw her all over Facebook, Chad. If you had a girlfriend, you should have told me. I'm not into home wrecking, and I'm not an idiot, either. You must have known I was going to figure it out." Rachael sent the texts, and then, she proceeded to write the same thing on his Facebook wall.

"I KNOW ABOUT SAMANTHA, AND I AM NOT AN IDIOT!"

Well, that posting got a huge response that went like this:

"Wow! You told him! LOL!"

"We all know about Samantha, she's been his friend since grade school!"

"Who are you anyway?"

"Some crazy bitch! LOL!"

"Yeah, who are you anyway, psycho?"

"Ummmm, she's 'Not AN IDIOT' LOL!!!"

And the digs and embarrassment went on and on... until Chad deleted the post.

Obviously, Chad never spoke to Rachael again.

His View

"When I met Rachael, I was really ready for a relationship. I had been through a couple of girlfriends where something just wasn't clicking, and I really wanted a girlfriend. When I met Rachael, we hit it off immediately—at a dentist's office no less. From the moment I saw her, I felt a strong connection to her. She was different than other girls. I couldn't wait to get back from my trip and spend time with her. I thought everything was going great until that night when she called me and I was out with my friends. Maybe I shouldn't have answered her call, but I wanted to talk to her even though I knew that my phone was about to die any minute. Because she had been at work, I had waited all day to talk to her. It was hard to hear because it was so loud where I was, and we were celebrating my friend Samantha's surprise engagement. I didn't even get a chance to tell her that my phone was going to die any minute. All of a sudden, it sounded like Rachael was mad. Then, the next thing I knew she was gone, and my phone was dead.

"The next morning when I woke up. I had several text messages. Some were from Rachel, and others from friends saying, 'Man, who is that girl that wrote on your wall?' and 'Geez, where did you find that one?' and 'Dude, you have a stalker! LOL!' I logged into Facebook, and I couldn't believe it. Rachael had written this crazy message on my wall for everyone to see. This was a side of her that was a shock to me. I was embarrassed, humiliated, and really confused. I had no idea how Rachael had gone from being a very cool girl that I was looking forward to dating to some deranged girl, writing crazy stuff on my Facebook page. To tell you the truth, that side of her scared me, and after that, I wanted nothing to do with her. Who needs that kind of crazy in their life?"

The Reality

The answer is that no one needs crazy in their lives. There are hundreds of reasons that things don't work out sometimes, and therefore, there are many things in life that you cannot control. The one thing that you can control is you and your reactions to situations. As far as Rachael was concerned, Chad had no one else in his life except her. She didn't stop to think that Chad had a life and friends before he met her. The expectation that Rachael had was that since she breezed onto Chad's life, even though it was a brand new budding relationship, in her mind, Chad shouldn't pay attention to (or even speak to) any other women. It was unrealistic and completely irrational of her to get as angry as she did that Chad had female friends and corresponded with them on Facebook. In fact, jumping to Chad's Facebook page for answers instead of talking to him about the issue she was having was wacky in the first place. And, of course, it led her to nothing but misconceptions.

When you're newly in a relationship, it's smart to not let yourself get too involved and attached too fast. Keep your hopes and your expectations in check. The truth is that when you start dating someone new, there is a lot that you have to learn about his life—who his siblings are, who his friends are, or who he spends the majority of his time with, for example. Rachael and Chad were too early into their relationship for Rachael to expect to know everything about Chad, and they were also too early into their relationship for her to expect Chad to feel like he had to disclose everything about himself to her at the drop of a hat.

Inventing stories about the guy you're dating is a key sign that you're not keeping yourself in check—and going on sites like Facebook to spy can be the fast track to Irrationalville! If you've worked yourself up into a tizzy and feel compelled to play detective, get ALL of the facts before you jump off the deep end. If you are in a story-inventing mood and you see the pictures he's tagged in on Facebook, well, you can cook up any narrative you want. By doing so, it's easy to spiral out of control.

In reality, you know that everything he does is not an indication about some greater pattern in his life. Every girl he talks to isn't a potential date, nor is every girl that talks to him on Facebook a secret girlfriend. But once you're in that mode, it's hard to remind yourself of these things. It's important to remind yourself not to overanalyze and not to overreact. If you just have to spy, there is already something either seriously wrong with the relationship or you.

Are you stirring up drama where there doesn't need to be drama? You talk to friends who are guys that you know aren't potential dates, so why not apply that same logic when thinking about the people your guy comes in contact with in his day to day life? And how about this: why not treat your guy as you would any *guy friend*? You're not going to go crazy on your friends' ass; are you? I hope not.

If you feel yourself getting upset about something, imagine if a friend told you the same story that you're going through right now. "I saw a picture of him and this girl. Do you think something's up with them?" If a friend said that to you, what would you say to her?

You'd probably say, "She's probably just a friend. Don't sweat it!"

Try giving yourself advice as though you were an observer, not a participant. What would you say to that friend?   You—Sane You, Observer You—would probably tell her to take a deep breath, keep herself in check, and remember that overanalyzing, overreacting, and freaking out never ends well. You'd also probably tell her (or you'd want to tell her) that she's being an Irrational Bitch!

CHAPTER 10:

Momma Bitch

Hey, there! Where's your cute little guy? Oh, you don't have a kid? Hmmm... that's strange. I could have sworn...

Well, who's that child you're always talking about, then? The way you talk about helping him clean up his mess and take on more responsibilities, I figured that he was your son! What is he—your nephew or something?

Uh-oh, wait a second. Are you kidding? He's your what? He's not a child at all? In fact, he's the man-child you're DATING?! Then I'm afraid, my dear, that you might have become a Momma Bitch!

Oh, baby! Treating your boyfriends like they're your responsibility to "raise and take care of" is going to get you nowhere but ALONE.

What are you, Ms. Fix-it? Are you trying to repair a broken man who acts like a child?

❖ <u>Momma Alert—Take the TEST!</u>

Before you even take this test, let me give you a hint at the lesson we're going to learn here. Repeat this mantra after me: "The only boy I'm going to raise is the one I give birth to." Okay, we'll review that and repeat it again at the end so that we're sure you don't forget it.

Now, onto the test. First things first: the guy. I'll bet you've met *that* guy. We all have. You know, the guy that was:

- Cute
- Sexy
- Charming
- Unpredictable
- Elusive

Mmm-hmm! And that combination was enough for you right off the bat; wasn't it? Cute, sexy, charming, unpredictable, and elusive *do* tend to be a get out of jail free card! But once the magical lust dust started to settle, did you start to see signs that what was really laying in your bed was just a gorgeous, charming man-child?

Telltale signs a man is a man-child are the following:

- He doesn't *exactly* have a job, per say.
- He doesn't even have any job prospects.
- He doesn't have a car.
- He lives with a lot of roommates in a "man cave."
- Or worse, he lives with HIS MOM.
- He's completely disorganized.

So, you've identified and recognized that you had yourself a man-child. But what did you do next?

Okay, now, this one is multiple-choice: Once you noticed he didn't exactly have his act together, you thought the following:

a) *"Uh-oh, he's a hot mess. Turn and run, now!"*

b) *"Uh-oh, he's a hot mess. But, he's **so** cute, fun and sexy, I could help him become a better man. Maybe we can still live happily ever after!"*

c) *"Uh-oh, he's a hot mess. But, he's **so** cute, fun and sexy, I could help him become a better man. We'll live happily ever after! In fact, I'll adopt him!"*

Oh, boy... Should I even look? If your answer was B, DANGER! DANGER! And if your answer was C, you might be beyond my help!

Once these thoughts enter your mind, you should hit the gas and peel out of the parking lot—lest you fall into a rather unfortunate trap: if you don't get away from situations like this one, you are about to start raising a child. With it, you are about to become his new momma. And that, my friend, is not going to end well. It can't possibly end well! You know that, and yet, maybe you find that you are head over heels and totally sure that we can change him and create the perfect man!

If you tend to take on projects in your boyfriends, it's time you come to terms with the fact that to be in a healthy relationship, he can't be your project. Until you accept that, you're going to have repeated experiences of empty-nest syndrome. You will spend countless hours getting his life together for him, only to the have him resent you for doing it. He will then leave you for someone else with whom he has a clean slate. I know you don't want that!

�֎ <u>Stephanie</u>

Stephanie was an awesome girl. She was bright and creative; when her group of friends would go out, she was the life of the party. She was a very cool person. She set a standard amongst her friends; everyone wanted to be as laid back, fun, and level-headed as Stephanie. She had the perfect job. She owned a house. She traveled a lot. All in all, she had a great life.

Until...

One day, Stephanie met Mark. She met him at a cousin's wedding, and she was immediately into him. They started seeing each other and really hit it off.

Stephanie's cousin was not enthusiastic about the bubbling love, and she warned Stephanie about Mark, saying his life was a mess. He was a surfer with low paying odd jobs, and he was in the middle of a divorce. He was basically a big kid.

"He's not your type," Stephanie's cousin warned. "He's trouble."

Stephanie just rolled her eyes. She didn't believe in "types," and besides, she once had odd jobs too (in high school). *All it takes to be a functioning member of society is a little focus and a good woman,* thought Stephanie, *and I'm just that woman.* And so, Mark became Stephanie's project.

It wasn't long before Stephanie had moved Mark out of his dank, dirty apartment that he shared with a couple of other guys on the other side of town and into her house. Right away, Stephanie started putting pressure on Mark to find a stable job and get rid of his old clunker. So, without even realizing it, she gave him homework assignments. "The way to find a job is to apply for at least five a day!" She really believed her own advice, and she had only the best intentions. Nevertheless, homework is homework. In fact, many times while he was busy surfing waves, Stephanie was busy surfing the internet and applying for jobs on Mark's behalf.

Meanwhile, she began probing into Mark's past issues. He had terrible credit, so Stephanie got to work improving his credit score. Though his wife had left him years ago, their divorce had never been finalized. Stephanie got on the phone with an attorney and started handling the divorce for him. She even paid his outstanding parking tickets.

While trying to whip Mark's life into shape, Stephanie began to get very annoyed when she didn't feel he was "changing enough." She was constantly on him about his actions—surfing too much, making a mess around the house, not finding a job yet. Stephanie couldn't believe that after all of her hard work, Mark still wasn't transformed into a take-charge guy. She nagged and nagged, and they fought like cats and dogs because of it. The constant nagging and fighting made Mark feel inadequate; it was as if just by being himself, he was never doing anything right. Mark grew to resent Stephanie and her constant fixing of his problems.

After a lot of interviewing, Mark got job. Eventually, Stephanie did get Mark's credit score up, and she got his divorce finalized. Even with his new credit score though, Mark wasn't a changed man. He preferred to surf and then play video games in his spare time, which Stephanie nagged and nagged about. At last, Mark became totally fed up with Stephanie and how she made him feel.

With his brand new improved salary and credit score, Mark finally got himself a brand new truck. And at his new job, he also got himself a new girlfriend. Guess what happened next? He drove off into the sunset with his new girlfriend and his new truck far, far away from Stephanie, leaving her in his dust. Stephanie was left devastated.

His View

"What I liked best about Stephanie was that she wasn't like any other girl I had ever dated. She had it together, and I thought, 'Hey, that's the girl and the life I'd like to have.' And I got it. Everything was going great until I moved in with her. All of a sudden, I had 'responsibilities.' I never tried to give Stephanie the impression that I was a responsible guy. I mean, seriously, I never hid the fact that I like to spend my days surfing or that I was anybody else but me. Right after I moved in with her, she changed and started acting like my mom. Man, that was a turn-off—to the point that we stopped having sex. No sex and a woman who was trying to micromanage my life? I don't think so. So, okay I'll admit it: I let her fix my credit and help me finalize my divorce. Why not? But the truth is that I was already on the lookout for a new girlfriend. It was perfect timing. I had just gotten my divorce finalized, and I got my new truck. Then, I met Tiffany at work. She surfs. She's easygoing and fun, and she gets me. Sure, I feel a little bad leaving Stephanie, but she's smart and capable. I know she'll be fine."

The Reality

Just like every other woman who has tried the same thing before her, Stephanie thought she could change Mark. She was wrong. The only thing Stephanie accomplished was that she helped Mark improve himself so that he could have a better life with someone else.

Ladies, listen carefully: you cannot change who a man is. What you see is what you get. You are getting him as-is—the same way you get a car off a lot as-is. You can't walk onto a car lot, point to a junker, and proclaim "I'll turn it into a Ferrari!" You also cannot find a man who is one thing and think you're going to turn him into something else. Like Stephanie, many girls are under the impression that every man has the *potential* to be what they want him to be; he just needs HER help, that's all. And since the girl has a lot of success in life, she thinks that she can "train" her man to be that guy she has always wanted.

It's easy to let yourself slip into this habit; isn't it? You tell yourself that there are no perfect men out there, and because of that, you're never going to find someone who fits the true profile of your ideal man. It's easier on the surface to find a guy you really like and insert those missing qualities into him, right? No! It's time consuming and emotionally draining for both people involved when one of you is trying to change the other. It's also impossible!

There are two ways to approach breaking your need for mothering your man. First, and probably most difficult, if you have this inclination towards projects to begin with, you can accept the guy for who he is. If he's a loveable teddy bear, but he doesn't have a big dose of ambition, so be it. Love him for who he is. Somebody will, you know; why not have it be you?

Here's why not: because he's not the type of man you want. You know deep down that you want someone who is a take-charge man, who is a match for your own take-charge attitude.

Secondly, and this is actually the right answer to your problem: you need to start dating men who fit the profile of the kind of man you ultimately want to be with. Look for the qualities inside the man, rather than the qualities outside of the man. Stop dating the fixer-uppers! It may sound simple, but trust me—we've all forgotten it from time to time. Instead of trying to turn a guy into something he's not, live and let live; those guys will find a girl to whom their qualities are desirable. Meanwhile, you should know and be proud of your standards. Be clear with yourself about what you *really* want, and pursue men who fit that profile.

Now repeat the mantra after me: "The only boy I'm going to raise is the one I give birth to." Don't forget it!

CHAPTER 11:

Needy Bitch

PUT DOWN THAT PHONE! Do not text him again until he's responded to your last text. Do you hear me?! Incessant texting is a telltale symptom of the smart, fun, independent girl turned needy. This also includes incessant calling, incessant attention grabbing, incessant compliment fishing, and so on.

So many great women are sane and stable until a man enters the scene. Then, it's all downhill from there. Suddenly, their livelihood depends on the unwavering attention of their "man," and without it, they're pouty and desperate. And guess what? Too much of you, too often and too fast, will scare men and make them run for the hills.

It also throws off the balance of nature. Men like to hunt and pursue, so a little mystery is necessary on your part.

Seriously? Why is that phone still in your hand? No! Don't call him either! Don't text him. Don't call him. Period.

Uh-oh, you're still doing it...! Please, just STOP and read the following before you make that call.

❖ <u>Needy Alert—Take the TEST!</u>

Are you a secure great, stable woman, *until* you start dating someone? The following are some telltale signs that you just might be a Needy Bitch:

- You have to see him all the time.
- You text him constantly.
- You call him constantly.
- Your phone is always out and on the table when he's not around.
- You always need to be the center of attention.
- You crave validation from others.
- You can't make a decision on your own.
- You are helpless without a man.
- You only feel pretty or special when you're with a man.

If your sanity depends on whether or not the phone rings and he's on the other end of the line, girl, sit down. I have to tell you something. You're a whole lot of Needy Bitch.

Kim

Kim was thirty-six and couldn't remember the last time she had dated anyone over a few weeks. She envied her sister, Nancy, and Kim would often tell Nancy that she had found *the only good man* worth having.

Nancy would always smile, laugh, and say, "You'll find someone, someday. They are out there".

In fact, Nancy's husband Nick had set Kim up with several of his guy friends, but for some reason, Kim was never "wowed." Until, one day, Nancy set Kim up with Nate, a guy from her gym. Lo and behold, they hit it off, and they began to date.

Perhaps because she hadn't dated someone in so long, Kim fell for Nate hard and fast. They had only gone out about four times, when Kim started hearing wedding bells. She told her friends and her sister that she didn't want to be set up with anyone else—this was it. She even took down her online dating profile. Kim began referring to Nate as her boyfriend when speaking to family and friends, even though they had never even come close to having a discussion about being exclusive.

Kim would call Nate everyday on her way home from work, and if he didn't answer, she'd call back a few times until he did. If Nate called Kim back while she was on the other line with a friend, she would ditch the friend immediately to take Nate's call. After all, it was *very* important to Kim that she spoke to Nate every day, and if that meant talking when it was convenient for Nate, so be it. When they weren't on the phone, Kim would text Nate to see what he was up to. In the event that he didn't text back, she nervously waited until he did. It was as though Kim's life depended on correspondence with Nate, which was just plain weird—she had only known him for a couple of weeks!

After the fifth date with Nate, Kim made up her mind that she wanted to sleep with him in order to cement the fact that they were in a "relationship" and to move that relationship to the next level more quickly. That night, she got her wish, and as far as Kim was concerned, the "relationship" was consummated. She left Nate's house in the morning feeling victorious that now, they were surely boyfriend and girlfriend...

...Too bad Nate didn't see it that way.

Nate's perspective was that he and Kim had only gone on five dates, and he was just getting to know her—just like he was getting to know several other girls. Nate had never kept it a secret from Kim that he was still dating other people and that Kim was just one of them. He even told her that he wasn't ready to commit to a relationship yet—with anyone.

After they slept together, though, Kim *assumed* that had changed. However, since Kim never told Nate that she saw their sleeping together as a symbol that they were in an exclusive relationship, Nate rightfully went about his life as he had prior to their night of passion.

Kim started calling and texting Nate even more frequently than she had before they slept together, but

Nate didn't change his behavior at all post-sex. In Kim's eyes, Nate's behavior pre-sex was not nearly as attentive as it should be post-sex. Boyfriends should act different than guys who are casually dating you, after all! Kim quickly grew very annoyed with Nate.

Things got especially bad one night when Kim was arriving to a restaurant with friends. Surprise! Who did she pass on the way in? That's right! Nate—with another girl. It was awkward in an instant, and Nate kept the encounter very short, leaving with the girl as quickly as he could. Kim, however, immediately had a pit her stomach the size of a boulder. As soon as she was in the restaurant, she ran into the bathroom where she collapsed in a stall, crying. *"Why would he do this to me?"* she thought. She was still an absolute mess when one of the friends she was out with came in to check on her.

Once her friend convinced her to leave the restaurant bathroom and join the group at dinner, Kim started to freak out by texting Nate, calling him, and rehashing every single detail with her girlfriends an attempt to figure it all out. Finally, later that night, Nate called

Kim, and after she told him how angry and hurt she was, he let her know that he didn't feel he had done anything wrong. It wasn't as though they had talked about being exclusive. Furious and upset, Kim hung up the phone.

Unsurprisingly, Nate never called again.

His View

"Wow, I've never been through so much drama before! Kim knew we were just dating. I was always very honest about that. But, as each day passed, Kim started to be really clingy, and after we slept together, it got even worse. She started acting like I was her boyfriend. I'm not sure what I could have done differently. Maybe I should have never slept with her. She would always leave sweet messages or send funny, cute texts, but that wasn't ever going to change the fact that I wanted a casual relationship. Part of me realizes now that she actually thought if she called enough, sent me cute, sexy texts, and slept with me, that I would change my mind. But, as a guy, that is actually more of a turn-off than a turn-on."

The Reality

Was Nate a bad guy? No. Nate was a guy who was doing what guys do: date. They date several girls at the same time until they decide to only date one. However, you have no control over that. The only thing you have control over is you. And you will run them off by being desperate, and needy.

When a girl meets a guy, she should be on her best behavior and play it cool—or as long as she can. However, when she becomes smitten with a guy, she immediately wants to lock him into a committed relationship right away. And when this enters her mind, all rash and reason go out the window. She'll say and do whatever she *thinks* it will take to make him her boyfriend.

Kim thought, *"I should send him a text and say 'Hi!' to let him know I'm thinking about him."*

Kim thought, *"I should send him another text of my new haircut, so he can see how cute I look."*

Kim thought, *"To be in a relationship, you need to talk."* So, she'd drop anything to take Nate's call.

Kim thought, *"People in relationships have sex."* So, she jumped into bed before she was ready, thinking that it would mean forgoing everything Nate was telling her and would put them on the fast track to a relationship.

Nate picked up on how much importance Kim was putting on Nate's attention to her, and it freaked him out.

Women who act needy often read into everything a man does or doesn't do and convinces themselves that his every word or gesture has a deeper "meaning" and it usually doesn't. The drama is usually something that you've created in your own mind, based on your past experiences and fear. For example, does a guy who's not calling you every moment of every day mean he's not into you? Not necessarily. However, once you convince yourself it does, you *rely* on his call to feel good and stable about the potentially budding romance. If he doesn't call, you call him—constantly.

Do those phone calls solidify or even help the relationship? Nope! It just makes you come off as overly dependent upon someone you *just* started seeing. But if you just sit back and wait to see if he calls, if he texts or if he asks you out, it will help you determine if he is really into you or not. But, you stressing ad trying to push it along, will not help at all.

Being needy is never attractive. It is basically like saying, "Please, oh, please be my boyfriend! I'm desperate and lonely and I have no other options!" And, really, who wants to be with that bitch?! It's a major turn-off.

Men want women who have options, who are interesting, and who have their own lives. Independence is a winning quality in a woman, but also remember that it's a fine line, too. When you meet a guy you really like, *play it cool but not cold.* Let him know that you have a life outside of him, and always remember that things take time. Sure, there will be times that you might talk to each other every day, but it isn't necessary. Life won't end if he doesn't call you today, so don't lose it if he doesn't call. Stay calm, stay busy, and focus on your life. And when you feel compelled to call, text, or cling, stop that urge! DO NOT act on it.

Use this mantra that I find helpful: "If he doesn't want me, then it's his loss, and he's a fool!"

CHAPTER 12:

Obsessive Bitch

SPLASH! Oh, crap. It looks like yet another nice, once intelligent, once promising girl has done a nosedive into the obsessed pool. Lifeguard, are you over there? I could use a little help here. This girl's gone off the deep end. Oh, geez, I can't look. She's right over there. Do you see her? She's the girl thrashing around like a crazy person. Oh, and all that she's saying over and over and over again is her boyfriend's name. Poor thing. It's such a shame when that happens; we can almost never fish them back out.

❖ **Obsessive Alert—Take the TEST!**

Okay, it's sink or swim time! You like this guy. You really, really, *really* like this guy. Find out if that "really" is really just an obsession. Does this sound like you?

- You can't stop thinking about him.

- You can't stop talking about him. You've even told the postman.
- You're already planning your wedding in your head.
- You're dreaming of him every minute.
- You find yourself constantly wondering what he's doing.
- You're fixated on why he's not calling.
- You can't focus on anything else.
- You're you starting to drive your friends nuts.

Here's an important question, and this is the killer...

- Are you are texting and calling him before he has a change to text or call you?

If you answered yes more than no, get a grip, girl. This could be a bumpy ride!

There was a universe before he came into your life, and there will be a universe after he leaves your life, which he certainly will do if you are doing nothing but obsessing over him—trust me. I've seen it happen to more than one girl. Hell, I've been that girl! You get involved with a guy. You fall off the deep end, and suddenly, you only have a one-track mind for this new dude. Before you know it, you are on autopilot, and you've programmed yourself to think about one thing and one thing only. The question amongst your friends and family becomes, "Who stole her brain?!" And the one and only answer to **every** question after that is, "Oh, yah, it's that new guy she's dating."

Obsessive women lose touch with reality, because in their reality, the world revolves around any man they like, date, or marry.

✖ Jen

Jen went on one date when the Peter bug bit her. Suddenly, everything was Peter this and Peter that. They had only been dating a couple of weeks when Jen's friends were already tired of the name Peter. "What do you think Peter's doing right now?" "When do you think Peter will call me?" "Do you think I should call Peter?" Peter! Peter! Peter!

Jen was always available for Peter whenever he called, because she constantly held her phone in her hand, waiting for it to ring.

When Peter would ask Jen if she wanted to get together on a weekend, she would say, "Absolutely! When? I am free both days." She even said this when she had preexisting plans with a friend! She was obsessed with and Peter and intent on seeing him every minute of the day.

As their relationship grew, Peter was literally all that Jen ever thought about or talked about. She pretty much defined her days according to what she and Peter did. So, when her friends would say, "What did you do this weekend, Jen?" She would answer, "Well, Peter bought us lunch, and then Peter and I saw a movie." Peter! Peter! Peter!

It wasn't long, though, before Jen's obsession with Peter went from loving to nitpicky. Like most people, Peter was not perfect. Sometimes he'd forget to wash a dish immediately after eating a sandwich, or he'd leave the toilet seat up. Jen, whose main focus in life was –

you guessed, it—Peter, would notice and was intent on analyzing every little thing Peter did. Then, she would relay all of these details to her friends. "Can you believe that Peter just left dishes sitting there like that?" "Why would Peter be such a slob as to leave the toilet seat up like that?" She would overanalyze each of these actions, and wonder aloud what it meant about Peter as a whole and what kind of person he was. She would convince herself that his even him leaving the toilet seat up meant that he obviously didn't care about her enough.

Jen's friends, frankly, didn't care why Peter did the things he did. They really were just sick of hearing about Peter.

Jen was so focused on every little thing he did—good and bad. Everything he did right, she talked about it, thought about it, and told all of her friends about it. Everything he did wrong, she talked about it, thought about it, and told all of her friends about it. Peter, meanwhile, couldn't deal with her constantly telling everyone every little detail of what he did and didn't do, so they started bickering. Then, she'd tell everyone about that, until finally Peter just couldn't take it anymore.

Yet, the most amazing thing was that once Jen and Peter broke it off, her obsession didn't stop. Her friends had hoped for sweet relief from the name "Peter," but instead, Jen's focus only got worse. For months and months, Jen continued to talk about Peter and all he had done wrong while they were dating. She would obsess over tiny details of what she perceived his new life to be, and she would talk endlessly about how terrible a person he was for getting involved in a life beyond Jen. Meanwhile, Jen was still alone, not coping, not moving forward, and not finding a new boyfriend.

His View

"Jen! Jen! Jen! Oh, man, I felt like I was living under a microscope. She told her friends EVERYTHING about me. Our relationship had no privacy whatsoever. And Jen, who was so fun and free spirited when I met her, became obsessed with me and with our relationship. I was embarrassed that everyone knew all of our personal details. And every time I saw her friends, they would give me a weird look. It was all very uncomfortable for me.

"Where did the Jen I met go? Was it something I did? She told me it was all my fault that our relationship ended, because I did this wrong or that wrong. The only thing I wish I had done is end it sooner than I did."

The Reality

In obsessing over Peter, Jen made him the center of her universe, and she gave up her own identity in the process. She put everything aside for Peter and made him her entire focus: the Earth, moon, and stars. In doing so, she created an image of Peter that was the "perfect man," but when Peter was imperfect, Jen was unable to deal with the fact that he was human, not super human.

No one will ever be able to provide you with the solutions to your problems. No ONE individual should hold that power over you. It's up to you to have a fulfilling life that sustains you and makes you complete. You DO NOT need anyone to complete you. You must be complete, strong, and fulfilled on your own before and during a relationship with a man. Jen clearly became obsessed with Peter, giving up her autonomy and ultimately her sanity.

By putting your entire focus on one man, you're creating the expectation that he will fulfill you completely. In reality, people need many different types of relationships in their lives to feel complete. We need friends, parents, siblings, family members, coworkers, bosses, teachers and neighbors—each person in our life brings something new to the table and gives us well-roundedness and emotional fulfillment. For many people, their spouse is a big factor in that equation. Spouses and children tend to take up a major part of the love we have to give, and they contribute to a major portion of the love we receive. However, you can love your husband completely and think he's the most wonderful specimen on Earth and still have fulfilling friendships and a life.

Lastly, and perhaps most importantly, when you're obsessing over a guy, you're losing yourself and who you are in your obsession. Why do you think he wanted to go on a date with you in the first place? Because of your uncanny ability to focus on the way he breathes? It's more likely he wanted to get to know you for who you are—your interests, your intelligence, and your wit. A healthy, sustainable, fun relationship is made up of two whole people—each of whom bring their own interests, opinions, and strengths to the relationship. Having interests outside of the relationship—quality time with friends, hobbies, and work—make you a well rounded person and gives you insight and intrigue to bring to the table.

If you are letting your whole life revolve around one thing, any one thing only, then you don't really have a balanced life; do you? If you've become obsessed with your man and your relationship, well quite frankly, that's not healthy! If this sounds like you, then you need to stop being obsessive, give him space, and keep your own life busy and full.

And please, stop sharing way too much with your friends! I assure you that they would much rather hear about the new charity you're working with or that great book you just read. Lose the obsession and get a new passion. Remember, the healthy balance that you maintain in your friendships and your life will contribute to an emotionally successful relationship with your partner.

CHAPTER 13:
Picky Bitch

Okay, so, get this: a guy and a girl are on a first date, and the guy says, "Can I have a little bit of your salad?" Before the girl even answers, she watches in slow motion as his fork comes across the air, over the table, lands in a piece of lettuce, lifts the lettuce off of her plate, and plants it directly into his mouth. Like a siren at a nuclear plant, loudly in her mind, she hears: DEAL BREAKER ALERT! DEAL BREAKER ALERT! DEAL BREAKER ALERT! Disgusted, she thinks in her mind, *Please, please let this date end. I cannot ever see this guy again! His manners are awful!*

Wow. A gross exaggeration, or are we onto something here?

Should I even bother to mention that the Salad Taster was also a single doctor, who has developed a revolutionary procedure, and because of it, he has helped many children around the world? No? Not worth even *mentioning*? It's not even possible that you'd *consider* labeling this girl ridiculous for writing him off for one little salad incident?

Picky Bitches, listen up! If you're tossing out a good guy for a minor infraction, then I recommend that you find your nearest cat shelter and begin the hoarding process right away. And I hope you're not allergic, as you will need them for their unconditional love in your very lonely senior years.

But, wait! Let's not overreact. Maybe you're not a Picky Bitch at all. Maybe you just have certain standards that need to be met. Hmmmm. Well, let's find out...

❖ Picky Alert—Take the TEST!

You're a Picky Bitch if you refuse to date him and you agree with most of the following statements:

- You hate his shoes.
- You're appalled by his manners.
- He picked the wrong restaurant.
- He isn't as cute as your last boyfriend.
- He's older than you expected.

- You find his job is boring.
- You think he's too goofy.
- He's under 6 feet tall.

Did any of those stand out to you as reason enough to not accept a second date with a guy? How many? Extra points if you thought that ANY of those reasons was enough to turn down even a first date with a guy!

Go ahead. Add it up! Uh-oh! Do you have more "true" than 'false" answers? We're definitely heading towards crowning you Little Miss Picky Bitch and you being permanently single; aren't we?

Let's see, though. Have you ever:

- Decided a guy wasn't right for you because he gave you a gift that totally wasn't your style?
- Hyper-focused on a potentially annoying quirk in a guy, rather than try to see any positives in him whatsoever?
- Been completely turned off because of what he was wearing?

Who do you think you are? Heidi Klum? No, she's got a husband. Gisele? No she's got a husband too. Wait, I know. Do you think you're Angelina Jolie? No, she has kids and a long-term partner. None of those women could be you, because you're alone. But you've got yourself convinced that you're such a catch that everyone's just intimidated by you, and *that's* why you're alone, right? Hmmm, that's weird, because Angelina, Heidi, and Gisele are pretty damn intimidating and *they're* not alone. So, what gives?

Do you ever wonder why you're single? Well, do you think you might be single because *you* aren't giving anyone a chance?

Lynn

Lynn was in her thirties, had a great job, and a big group of friends—most of whom were already married, except Lynn. She just didn't get it; why could everyone else find someone but not her? Meanwhile, every time Lynn went out on a date, the guys were totally weird and had more quirks than they did charm. She told her friends constantly, "You guys have all the luck!"

Lynn's friends were always trying to set her up on dates, and finally, her friend Dawn was sure that she had found the perfect guy for her. Chris was sweet, had a great job, had been in long-term relationships before, and was looking for someone to get to know, to spend time with, and hopefully settle down with. Dawn was sure Chris and Lynn had enough in common that they would hit it off, so she set it up.

The night that Chris and Lynn went out, things started off great. Chris was immediately attracted to Lynn, and she could tell that he was really into her. She had her charm turned up to 100%, and Chris was eating it up with a spoon. Their date went great, and Lynn was thrilled when Chris asked her out again.

Lynn was really excited for her second date with Chris, and she even went out and bought a new outfit for the occasion. She left her house confident that she was looking her absolute hottest—a suspicion that was confirmed when she saw more than one guy check her out on her way to the restaurant. She was feeling so good that she was *especially* surprised when she saw what Chris wore to the date.

Bad ugly jeans and dad sneakers? Odd, Lynn thought. But, once they were sitting down their table, having dinner, it wasn't as though Lynn could actively see the ugly jeans and shoes. She put it out of her mind, and Chris was just as charming as he had been on the first date. Lynn had nearly forgotten about his lack of fashion know-how by the time they left the restaurant.

At the end of their second date, Chris was so taken with Lynn that he asked her on the spot if she'd like to go out again that weekend. Lynn said yes, and they agreed to meet for drinks before grabbing dinner that Saturday night. Well, between the second and third dates, Lynn couldn't stop thinking about those dorky jeans and sneakers that Chris had worn on the second date! She began to wonder, *If he's that clueless about what to wear to a date, is he clueless in life as well?"*

With Lynn's obsession with what Chris wore on the second date, it should come as no surprise that as soon as she arrived to the third date, Lynn began inspecting what Chris was wearing. Unfortunately for both of them, he was wearing the same jeans, and though he was wearing better shoes this time, he wore a shirt that just looked a little out dated.

He once again looks like he took a page out of the dorky dad handbook, thought Lynn.

Although Chris was just as charming, kind, and smart as he had been on the previous two dates, Lynn had pretty much already made up her mind that it could never work because of his horrible taste in clothes. After that date, she told Chris that she didn't think they should continue to see each other.

A few weeks later, when Lynn's friend Dawn asked her why it hadn't worked out with her and Chris, Lynn confessed, "Uuugghh! I couldn't stand his clothes! He was just so nerdy! I was embarrassed to be seen with him dressed like that!"

Dawn burst out laughing, and she told Lynn that when she had met her husband years earlier that he too didn't have much of a sense of style. "Once we had been dating a while, I took him shopping and made him over! It's much easier to find a good guy and just give him a little fashion help than it is to try and tame one of those super stylish guys, hoping that he becomes husband material. In my experience, it never really worked that way."

Too bad Lynn wrote Chris off before she got that great advice.

His View

"I thought Lynn was great! She was nice, charming, and fun. She seemed like the kind of girl that I would love to get to know. I could have seen myself spending a lot more time with her and maybe even getting serious with her. I would have loved to have gotten the chance to have known her better."

The Reality

It seems like Chris is a pretty nice guy, and that he was really into Lynn. Of course, Lynn didn't really give herself a chance to be liked by him for long. Instead, Lynn let herself get hung up on one detail, and from there, she spiraled into her normal routine: she began examining Chris under a magnifying glass and nitpicked the tiniest of little details. Lynn was so busy focusing on what was "wrong" with Chris that she was unable to notice what was right with him: he really liked her, and he was smart, kind, and charming. Lynn refused to see past his clothes, and that was that.

When you're being a Picky Bitch, you're not giving a guy a chance, and you're also reading far too deeply into every little thing he does. When you meet someone for the very first time, it's natural to look at dates with a careful eye, but if you nitpick about every little detail and you think that that one thing defines him and who he is, then you'll always find something wrong with everyone and always end up alone. Why? Because *people have quirks and no one is perfect.*

When you find yourself on *yet another* date where the guy was too short, too tall, too thin, or had a weird tone in his voice that you just didn't like, take a step back and remind yourself that being overly picky about those types of things isn't fair to him—or to you. If you're too picky, you're setting your dates up for failure. There is simply no way that the men you go out with could possibly live up to your impossible standards of perfection. By the way, I have to ask: are you perfect?

If you want to find a boyfriend, you need to adjust your perspective on dating. Instead of focusing on what about him *isn't* in line with your idea of perfection, look for things about him that *are*. Go into each date looking for positive qualities in the man you're out with, and don't even let yourself focus anything but the positive. Even if he does have things about him that you don't think are perfect—and trust me, he will— don't think about them. Pretend that imperfection doesn't exist. In other words, *give the guy a chance!*

There is no man you're going to find, anywhere, that's going to be everything on your list. What human being could possibly hit every single criteria of perfection that the other person has for them? No one! Would you? Think about it. What if the guy you were going out with was running down a checklist of superficial "perfect girl" qualities, and what if he was determining which you possessed and which you didn't? Wouldn't you feel like you were under a microscope and like you weren't being given a fair chance? And, yes, ladies, some guys do that. In fact, many, many guys do that, and those are the guys that stay perpetually single as well.

I've said it before, and I'll say it again, if you want a boyfriend or a husband, you *have* to be open minded. A closed mind will get you nowhere. Who cares if he asks you for coffee rather than dinner? Who cares if he does yoga and you think it's wimpy? I'm sure the picky list could go on, but I'll stop with those two examples.

A guy might ask you to coffee, not because he's cheap, but because he's nervous. Or, may he really is cheap, but give him the benefit of the doubt until it's otherwise proven. And a man who does yoga? Well, Sting, the singer does yoga, and he doesn't seem at all wimpy to me. The point is this: don't judge too harshly, be open-minded, and dig deeper within yourself before tossing out the good guys like they're yesterday's news.

CHAPTER 14:

P.I.T.A. Bitch

Rough day for poor little you? The cashier at the supermarket double charged you for that can of refried beans, and you had to wait until the manager could come and override her mistake?, But you handled it well. Stomping your foot, huffing, and rolling your eyes. You go girl. And then at dinner, *of course,* the waiter at the restaurant didn't take *your* dinner order first. (*How dare he?!*) Oh you poor sweet little darling!

Yikes! Wait just a moment, here. Are you royalty or something? Did Daddy always call you his "little princess," and somewhere along the line, you became convinced that you actually *are* a princess? Well, suffice it to say that if you'd feel embarrassed *dressing* like a princess in public, you should probably feel embarrassed acting like one, too.

If you tend to make demands of your friends, the people you date, and the world at large, you're probably a P.I.T.A. Bitch: Pain in the Ass. But before we go too far, let's make sure that this is the proper diagnosis for you.

❖ P.I.T.A. Alert—Take the TEST!

These are the tell tale signs that you might just be a pain in the ass:

- Do you always expect to have everything your way?
- Do you feel entitled to special treatment?
- Do you value your own time, but no one else's?
- Do you embarrass your friends at restaurants by wanting to be waited on hand and foot?
- Do you expect the men you date to be mind readers?
- Do you often pout or throw hissy fits because things don't go exactly the way you wanted them to?

How did you do on the test? Uh-oh, did someone just realize that she might just be a P.I.T.A. Bitch? If you failed this test and you often find yourself pouting because things aren't going your way, WATCH OUT! You are a Pain in the Ass, and that will *definitely* be one ass that stands in the way of you getting a boyfriend.

✠ <u>Summer</u>

Summer was once on track for the perfect "white picket fence" lifestyle. She married her high school sweetheart, Dan, who had a great job. Summer and Dan fell into a very affluent lifestyle very young, and before she was thirty, Summer was accustomed to having only the nicest things. She and Dan lived in a gorgeous new construction home, which was furnished with only the best furniture from the most posh stores. Of course, Summer's wardrobe matched the style of her home, and it was also top of the line.

When the economy got rough, like many professionals, Dan lost his job. Though he was being called in for interviews consistently, Dan was always interviewing against other qualified candidates—some of whom were even more qualified than he was. Dan was trying as hard as he could, but the market was rough.

Although they were staying afloat, Dan and Summer had to cut back on their spending drastically. But, cutting back meant that Summer could no longer buy the lavish clothes she wanted, and it also meant canceling Dan and Summer's planned vacation to a luxury resort in the Bahamas.

Summer began to feel that she and Dan were no longer the "people they once were," and after months of arguing, unkind words, and hurt feelings, Dan and Summer's relationship was on very rocky ground. Finally, she decided she wanted a better lifestyle and was no longer interested in even trying to repair the marriage.

Finding herself back on the market, Summer decided to have even higher standards this time around. Summer made up her mind; she was going to find someone who she knew would bend over backwards for her no matter what. She wanted a guy who would buy her the nicest things, who would take her to the nicest resorts, and who would always drop whatever he was doing to spend time with her. Summer was stunningly beautiful, and she practically had men lining up around the block to date her. But, even though men would jump through hoops to get with Summer, they didn't stick around very long.

Finally, one boyfriend, Steve, seemed like he had a high tolerance for the more material side of Summer's demands. Summer's friends watched in awe and thought it actually might work out between Steve and Summer. Steve had the bank account to buy things from Cartier and Tiffany's, so Summer always got what she wanted. She only wore clothes from the top designers, and Steve bought them for her. Summer wanted portions of Steve's home redecorated to fit her style, and he went for it.

What Steve couldn't stomach after many months, though, was the more emotional side of Summer's P.I.T.A. tendencies. If Steve didn't drop absolutely everything for Summer, she'd lose it. Summer called Steve at work one day, and when his assistant said he was in a meeting that she couldn't pull him out of unless it was an emergency, Summer yelled at Steve's assistant about how Steve should always be available for her—emergency or not. And that was no match for the words she gave Steve when she finally got on him the phone!

The final straw came on the day of the Super Bowl, which Steve considered the most important event of the year. He was especially excited this year, because his hometown team playing. He arranged a viewing with his friends from work to watch the game. Summer wanted to come, but Steve told her that it was tradition every year that this one event was a "guys only" gathering. Summer wasn't happy about it, pouted a bit, and finally realized that it was nonnegotiable.

That night, right around kickoff, Summer called Steve. Steve answered, but he was very brief, reminding Summer that the Super Bowl was on and that his buddies were over to watch the game. Still not getting (or caring) "what the big deal with football was," and completely annoyed that Steve rushed her off the phone the way he did, Summer called Steve back and told him that they needed to talk.

Steve excused himself from the game to speak with Summer, who started to completely fly off the handle.

She was crying, and she accused Steve of putting his friends before her. As the conversation continued, she accused Steve of not caring about her at all. "If you really loved me, you'd take my call no matter what was going on, not shove me off for some stupid game with your stupid friends!"

Steve tried to stand his ground, but he was very frustrated with Summer. Plus, he was missing something that he had told Summer, more than once, was important to him. Summer continued to push, asking Steve why football was so much more important to him than she was. Finally, in the heat of it, Steve told Summer that she was a materialistic, spoiled brat and that he wasn't going to put up with it anymore. His friends cheered in the background—but not for the game!

The good news was that his team won the Super Bowl, and Steve got his balls back. The bad news was that he missed most of the game, and Summer was back on the market again.

His View

"There were parts of our relationship that were great, and when she wasn't being—excuse the term—a bitch, there was a lot I really liked about her—mostly her looks. She was beautiful, so I was willing to put up with her attitude. But, after a while I just couldn't really stomach her demanding personality anymore. If I didn't call her three times a day, she said I wasn't spending enough time thinking about her. If I didn't get her flowers, then I didn't love her. If I wouldn't drop everything I was doing to cater to some whim she was having, I was a horrible person, and our relationship was doomed because of it. After a while of going through enough of that back-and-forth, eventually, it doesn't matter what she looks like or how good in bed she is; it's just not worth it anymore."

The Reality

The relationship was doomed, but it wasn't because of Steve not wanting (or being able to) to drop everything for Summer anytime she demanded his presence. Steve and Summer's relationship was doomed because

Summer was a spoiled P.I.T.A. Bitch. It was only a matter of time before Steve was going to be fed up and ditch Summer.

If you think that everyone should drop everything all of the time to cater to all of your needs, then it might be time to get you a much needed dose of reality.

The reality is that a man will put up with your demands, if you're really, *really* hot, but he'll still only put up with it until he's slept with you enough times. Then, he'll eventually have enough sex with the Pain in the Ass Bitch, and he will be gone.

The number one thing that men crave other than a girl being physically attractive is that she is easy going. A man wants a woman who will go with the flow. If you throw a fit every time something doesn't go exactly the way you wanted it to, that is the opposite of "easy going." Before long, any guy who spends any time with you will realize that you are beyond difficult. And while you drag your man by the arm and pout because you've been to *three stores so far and they don't have those blue Manolo Blahniks*, that guy is going to be plotting his getaway. He will have had it with your spoiled bitch routine, and soon, he will be gone, in search of a girl who is fun and laid back.

If you tend to crave—no, if you tend to *need*—perfection in absolutely every aspect of life, you are probably a P.I.T.A. Bitch. If you make your friends and your man feel like nothing is ever good enough, it will make everyone around you feel like they are walking on eggshells. Walking on eggshells does not lead to walking down the aisle; it leads to walking away. No one wants to put up with someone who's constantly whining and unsatisfied, especially that delicious guy that you wish was your boyfriend.

If you are a high-maintenance P.I.T.A. Bitch, I urge you to take a step back and think about yourself as a girlfriend. If you were a guy, would you date you? How would you if feel the gifts and accolades you gave to someone were never quite good enough? Personally, everyone I know would run far, far away from that joy-kill.

Let's be clear. It's not about quantifying the things a man can buy you, like Louis Vuitton bags or diamond necklaces from Cartier. P.I.T.A. Bitches tend to also quantify the simpler things in a relationship, such as how often a guy shows her that he is thinking of her with phone calls or flowers, how much time he spends with her, or how many times a day he hugs her.— The same way Summer acted as though Steve wanting time with his friends to watch a game meant that he didn't love her, P.I.T.A. Bitches count things like affection as currency, and they act as though a guy has to spend enough of that currency to buy her love. **Love can't be bought** with time and attention or with material things.

If you want to find love, true love, you have to be willing to give before you take—and not expect anything in return. Not appreciating what he does and instead focusing on what he needs to do to prove he loves you just makes you an impossible-to-please Pain in the Ass Bitch.

If you find yourself incapable of appreciating the little things, then maybe you should get out and do a little philanthropic work. Volunteer at a nursing home, an animal shelter, or at a children's hospital. That way, you can see life from a more humble perspective. Maybe if you let a little humility and understanding into your life, you might realize that there is much more to life than your own shallow needs. Be appreciative, be grateful, and, most of all, take a deep, breath and just go with the flow.

CHAPTER 15:
<u>Self-Centered Bitch</u>

Imagine a clear, sparkling, starry sky. Ah, endless stars—bright, dreamy, tranquil. Maybe there's some soothing music playing, too. Yes, yes, soothing music and stars—imagine it. Feel the floating quality of that beautiful, endless sky. Now, picture the planets that are amongst those stars, orbiting, orbiting. They each have their own paths, and they circle around one, big, shiny star—the center of it all. The center star is mighty, bright, and beautiful. It's warm. Now, imagine that all of those planets are the people in your life; they're orbiting, orbiting. The planets seem very small and insignificant, as they rotate around that one, big, giant star. Now picture yourself. Where do you fit in?

Whoa! Wait just a second! Stop the soothing music! Did you *really* just place yourself in the center, where the sun should be? I was going for "love and compassion" as the center star, not *you!* Come on! What are you? A Self-Centered Bitch?

❖ <u>Self-Centered Alert—Take the TEST!</u>

See for yourself:

- Do you only relate to situations as they relate to you?
- Do you get confused when everyone in the world doesn't have the same attention span for your stories about your day as your parents do?
- Do you think that what you did today is the only thing that *really* matters?
- Do you think that what you ate for dinner last night is newsworthy?
- Are you under the impressions that everyone should receive updates about your every move?
- Does it bore you when others are talking and the conversation doesn't involve you?

Uh-oh! Is someone Self-Centered? Thanks Twitter for making us all believe that strangers care about what we ate for breakfast! Are you *honestly* so egotistical that you really think people want to hear every little detail of your life, all the time? Well, while you're blabbering on and on about your favorite superstar (yourself), what do you think your friends are doing? They are praying for a natural disaster, while rolling their eyes and looking the other way. And, do you know what's worse? What do you think your DATES are doing? Let me go out on a limb and make the wild guess that what they *aren't* doing is asking you out again.

If you choose to be Self-Centered, you don't need a boyfriend; you need a dog who will love you unconditionally and who will hang on your every word. But, since this book is not called *Stop Being a Bitch and Get a Dog,* let's get into how to fix your little self-obsession problem—and fast.

✠ Jessie

Jessie was eager to find her soul mate—so much so that she looked for him everywhere. The topic of men and dating was always in the forefront of her mind.

Caroline, Jessie's friend and coworker, was her constant sounding board. Jessie was always gushing about the details of her life to Caroline. The two women had met years earlier, and Caroline had unwittingly fallen into the role of playing "therapist" for Jessie.

Caroline was a girl in her thirties who had it all together. She had a great job, and she was engaged. And although she herself had been off of the dating scene for quite some time, Caroline was never far from thinking about it because of Jessie, of course. All day, every day, Caroline smiled and nodded as Jessie regaled her with the day-to-day news of every aspect of her life—*especially* dating. So even though Caroline hadn't been on a date for years, she felt like she had. Jessie gave her every single detail, from what she wore to what he smelled like to what his kisses were like— and more. With Jessie, the TV was only ever turned to one station: "Jessie TV." Like it or not, Caroline was the captive audience. If the conversation ever veered off Jessie and onto Caroline and her life, it didn't for long.

One day, Jessie was being set up with Josh, a man that her cousin had set her up with. She was especially excited for this date. Therefore, Jessie talked Caroline's ear off at lunch about everything she had heard about him. According to her cousin, Josh was extremely attractive; he had a great job; and his hobbies and interests were very in line with her own.

That night, when Jessie got to the date, she immediately saw that the hype was true: Josh was indeed absolutely gorgeous. Jessie fluffed her hair, licked her lips, and told herself, *Let's do this!*

But, by the time their dinner had been served, Jessie was already starting to feel fatigued. Josh hadn't stopped talking about himself—once! He hadn't complimented her at all.

Why isn't he mentioning how great I look? Jessie thought.

While Josh blabbered on about his job, his educational background, and even his previous girlfriends—most of who were models—Jessie had completely tuned him out.

Can you believe this guy? she asked herself. *It's like he doesn't even realize I'm here—he's on a date with himself!*

Josh thought Jessie was a great listener and wanted to see her again, but Jesse was absolutely not interested.

The next day at work, she spent most of the morning rehashing the event and telling her friend Caroline every detail of the disastrous date. "He talked about nothing but himself! He didn't even ask one question about me, and I'm, like, hello? What about me? I'm right here!"

Caroline, as usual, patiently nodded and listened.

His View

Rather than hear from Josh, who I'm sure is too busy staring at his own reflection in the mirror to think about Jessie, let's hear from Caroline:

"Oh. My. God! I wish I could convince Jessie to date this guy; it sounds like she has finally found her match! Listen: I love Jessie. We've been friends and coworkers for years, but all that girl does is talk about herself!

Literally, all that she does is go on and on about her life, her dates, her problems, her hopes, and her dreams. I feel like her therapist. It comes as no surprise to me that no man has wanted to sign up for that! Sorry, but it's true. I think the reason Jessie didn't like Josh is because he didn't make her the center of his attention right away. Usually, she's able to dominate the conversation early enough that the guy has no choice but to make her the main focus. Of course, they almost never call her again, and she can never seem to figure out why..."

The Reality

In this situation, the world revolved around Josh, and Jessie couldn't stand it. But, did she attempt to turn the conversation around, to interject, or to get a word in edgewise? No, she did not, because she was too preoccupied with why Josh wasn't paying enough attention to her. Did Josh notice? Nope! He was too busy going on and on about himself.

The story of Jessie's date with Josh couldn't be more perfect, because we got to see how much it irked Jessie to have a taste of her own medicine. Josh was a Self-Centered Bitch!

But, enough about Josh—let's look at Jessie and how she's completely unaware of what she's been doing on dates and even in her friendship with Caroline.

Relationships are built on a mutual interest in one another. If you have no interest in anything but yourself, a relationship isn't going to happen—not a true one, anyway. Jessie's friendship with Caroline is complicated. Caroline says she's Jessie's friend, but it's obvious that she resents her and begrudges having to play her therapist. I'm not sure if the friendship would even last if they didn't have to work together. Caroline says it herself—she knows that her friendship with Jessie is a one-way street, and she can't imagine a guy signing up for that. Caroline is on-point here.

Though Jessie and Caroline may be casual friends, the relationship Jessie is looking for when she goes out on dates—a romantic relationship—is typically a very large part of one's emotional life.

People expect and need mutual admiration and respect in any relationship. Emotional support that is fuelled by a genuine interest and care for the wellbeing of another person is necessary if you want a healthy relationship. You should provide laughter at their jokes and a shoulder to cry when needed. A healthy relationship means contributing to each other's sense of strength and comfort in the world at large.

As we have talked about before, dating is a way of sizing people up for their partnering potential. You glean signs, hints, and clues as to what you're in for down the road. Whether you like it or not, you are being judged on who you are based on how you behave and present yourself on a date. It's important—as it was to Jessie—that your date has some interest in you, what you want, who you are, and how you feel. When you go on a date and talk about nothing but yourself, though, it sends the message to your date that your biggest concern in life is you and you alone. This is a huge red flag, and it sends the message that you might not be a very nurturing or caring person. If someone takes no interest in you, you assume they don't like you that much or that they don't have much of an interest in your wellbeing.

What do you take from that experience? Well, usually, you would come to the obvious conclusion that someone who doesn't care about your wellbeing wouldn't make a good long-term partner, or even a good friend, and you would write the person off.

It is great to have the confidence in yourself to know that you are strong, smart, and sexy. You're a real catch, and you know it! Confidence itself is a great quality, and it's an attractive one as well. However, having confidence doesn't mean that the sole focus of attention should always be on oneself. To get love, one must give love. It's as simple as that. It's important that you always stay in touch with reality about your place in the world and in a relationship.

If you have a tendency to be Self-Centered, it's a good idea to keep yourself in check. If you think this might be you, ask your friends to be completely honest with you and let them know you won't be mad (and you have to mean it) that you want to improve yourself.

And, on dates, make sure you're asking about him, who he is, and what he's up to. Remember that this date is just as much about you getting to know him as it is about him getting to know you. Although dating is about feeling out potential partners, it's not a job interview. You don't need to present a laundry list of positive qualities and past experiences.

Speaking of past experiences, please, please, please, whatever you do, DO NOT share heavy personal family drama or talk about your previous boyfriends and how great (or awful) they were. Men hate to hear about other men you've dated anyway. And this guy you just met does not need to know your entire history, nor does he need to know every little detail about your day.

Be a good conversationalist. Ask him questions about his interests, and get to know him. The dance of good dialogue is give and take, back and forth. Engage him, and be engaged. After all, it's not all about you! It's about you and him and the potential to be you + him.

CHAPTER 16:
Unavailable Bitch

Beware of Unavailable Bitch—she walks among us! She is misleading and dangerous, and she is ready to waste a whole lot of everybody's time—including her own. You'll have to look closely though, because the Unavailable Bitch looks and acts like many other girls. She looks like your friend, your neighbor, or even your sister! She could be hiding behind any corner, or worse—she could very well be the reflection in your own mirror.

❖ **Unavailable Alert—Take the TEST!**

- Are you usually pining away after men you can't have?
- Are you in search of the perfect guy, but he's never quite perfect enough?
- Do normal nice guys turn you off?
- Do you get a thrill out of taking someone else's guy?

- Does the thought of consistency with one man scare the hell out of you?
- Are most of the men you are attracted to immature?
- Are most of the men you're attracted to not interested in you?
- Are you running away from the good guys who *are* interested in you?

Well, if you said yes more than you said no, then unfortunately you are probably an Unavailable Bitch, and I would advise that you keep reading.

The Unavailable (or Commitment Phobic) woman is a person who—often in spite of herself—is not emotionally available for healthy, happy, harmonious relationships. The tricky thing is that it's easy for the unavailable gal to be elusive, even to herself, because she's single, and usually, she appears to be "actively looking" for The One. However, The One never seems to arrive. Instead, she falls for a whole lot of guys with whom it can't ever possibly work out.

Have you ever spent all of your time and energy hoping for attention and love from:

- The guy that's not ready for a commitment?
- The guy that lives halfway across the country?
- The guy who already has a girlfriend?
- The guy who's married?
- The guy who's married with kids?
- The drug addict, sex addict or alcoholic?
- The permanent playboy?

It was doomed from the start! What this commitment-phobe doesn't realize is that she picks these guys because *they are unavailable, just like her.*

What's the benefit to picking such unattainable men? It's very easy: the existence of a man whom she can never have allows the unavailable woman to have a long list of excuses—for herself and for others—by pinning the fact that it didn't work out on the guy instead of herself. In reality, she's not admitting that she is one Unavailable Bitch.

❉ <u>Monique</u>

Monique was always out on dates, and many times would amuse her good friend and colleague, Paul, by regaling him with comically woeful tales of her struggles with men. She always found something wrong with the men she dated. A lot of times, Monique would even jokingly refer to herself as the most unattainable bitch she had ever met. No one was good enough for Monique but a very select few.

Every couple of months, Monique would find a man that she was sure she must have. For instance: the UPS guy (married), the cool, sexy bartender (always high on something), or the new hot neighbor (gay). She'd go on and on about her interactions with these men and her approach to everlasting love with them, but, unsurprisingly, it never worked out.

Finally, one day, Monique showed up at lunch to squeal in joy about a guy that was seemingly unlike the others she had tried to date. Frank wasn't married; he wasn't high; and he wasn't gay. In fact, he was just a nice, forty-something guy who had a house, owned a successful business, and seemed pretty normal. He had never been married before, and neither had Monique. They had a lot in common.

"Really?" Paul asked, supportively. "That's great, Monique."

She nodded, smiled, and said, "Thanks!"

Things with Frank and Monique went fine. He knew all the hot spots, took her to the finest restaurants, knew exactly what to order, and said all of the right things. He was witty, charming, and very stylish. He had the perfect designer house and the very best car—he had the best of everything. He even gave Monique plenty of space. He wasn't constantly calling her or trying to cage her in.

Monique would go on and on about all of the exciting places that Frank would take her, and she gushed about their whirlwind romance to her loyal pal and confidant, Paul. Paul, meanwhile, secretly worried that although Frank did seem different in many ways to Monique's usual "type" of guy, he also had a lot of similarities to the guys she'd usually date. Paul wondered why Frank hadn't ever been in a long-term relationship before.

Monique told Paul that Frank had always just focused on his booming hotel business, so he just never had the time for a family, pets, or even houseplants. Paul asked Monique if she and Frank ever had meaningful discussions about life. Paul's biggest concern was that Frank seemed great at sweeping someone off their feet, but was there any real substance behind it? Monique brushed it all off and let herself get more involved with Frank. Soon, they slept together.

However, after they slept together, Frank was clear that he didn't want Monique to spend the night. Monique thought it was strange, but she obliged and went home. This happened time and time again, though, and finally, Monique asked Frank what was up. Frank explained that he enjoyed his freedom, his space, and *his bachelor pad.* He also said that he liked things the way they were between them and wanted to keep it that way. The problem was that Monique wasn't sure what he meant by "keeping things the way they were."

The more Monique pushed to get answers, the more distant Frank became. The more distant Frank became, the more Monique liked him. She turned to Paul for advice and a shoulder to cry on, but Paul was tired of hearing this same, old story: crying over a guy that she could never have.

Just about this same time, Paul met a great girl and decided to give his energy and time to her and their budding relationship. Monique was left to sort out her feelings for Frank on her own. Finally, after casually dating Frank and waiting almost a year for him to commit, Monique gave up and decided to move on.

His View

Here's what Frank had to say:

"I saw Monique from across the lobby at one of my hotels, and I was immediately attracted to her. So, like I do with the many beautiful women I see every day, I went over to her, struck up a conversation, and asked her out. We started dating, and it was great. She was fantastic, and the sex was mind-blowing. But, none of that changed the fact that I like my single life. I thought that was obvious from the beginning, but like most women I meet, Monique thought she could be the one to make me want to settle down. But, she couldn't, because I love my lifestyle. It's easy and casual, and I love the fact that I can have almost any beautiful woman that I want."

Meanwhile, here's what Paul had to say about Monique:

"I was crazy about Monique, but she never seemed to acknowledge me in a romantic way. It started out as a typical crush. I thought she was so pretty, so fun, and such a magnetic presence. We got along great, too. The best part of my day was seeing Monique. I asked her out soon after we met, but she made it clear she only wanted to be friends with me. Then, to make things worse, she was constantly going on dates with these guys who weren't good enough for her, or they didn't like her.

"She would call me for advice. I put up with that for a long time and had high hopes that maybe she would see that I was a great guy who really cared for her, but she didn't. So, I finally gave up. Over and over, it seemed to be a pattern: playing her usual mind games, the chasing, the flirting, and dating the guys that were obviously not right for her. Then sleeping with him and getting attached; she treated the whole dating thing like a game, time and time again.

"I guess I eventually realized that I didn't need to be involved with a girl like that. I had to stop talking to her as much as I used to in order for my life to move forward. If it wasn't going to work out, I had to take responsibility for my side of it and stop wasting my time wishing that she'd come around. I wanted a real relationship, and once I stopped wasting my energy on Monique, I'm happy to say that I finally have one."

The Reality

Paul is right. Monique wasn't ever going to see him as more than a friend. At no fault of his own—he could be the cutest, most charming, loving guy out there—but Paul was just too normal for Monique. Paul was the type of guy you marry and have a stable wonderful life with, and Monique like men who were unpredictable and edgy.

Even though Monique obsessed over the fact that she couldn't find The One, in reality, Monique wasn't ever looking for The One. Monique was playing just as many mind games with herself as she ever was with someone she was dating. And when she met Frank, she was fooling herself into thinking that this time—despite the obvious signs—it might work out.

The phrase "red flags" exists for a reason. There are certain things that really do stand in the way of a relationship working out. Primarily, it's that both people have to be on the same page and both need to be ready and available for a healthy relationship. The unavailable girl knows this down deep, but on the surface, she convinces herself that she is ready for the right guy. *This one is different.* She thinks this is one game she can win. This one will defy the odds, and it'll all work out in the end.

Why does she this to herself? Obviously, she's not ready for a relationship, so she gets herself in situations that she knows won't work out. She likes attention. She likes excitement, but for one reason or another, a real relationship is not in the cards at the moment. She's emotionally unavailable. Getting involved in situations that can't possibly work out is a form of self-preservation and a way to not take ownership of the fact that she isn't capable of a relationship right now. It's a mind game she plays with herself.

If you tend to go after unavailable guys, and you always find yourself in relationships that were doomed from the start, or aren't really relationships, you might just be commitment phobic.

And if you aren't yet being honest with yourself about the fact that it's you—not everyone else—that's standing in your way, take a step back and answer these questions:

- What do you really want right now?
- What about your life is working out?
- What isn't working?

- What role do you actually want a guy to play in your life right now?
- If you met the perfect man tomorrow, would you be ready to settle down with him?
- Are you actually available for a committed relationship?
- Does the thought of a "normal" stable relationship give you feelings of anxiety?

If a serious relationship isn't in the cards at the moment, the faster you identify that for yourself, the better. That way, you can stop leading guys on, stop letting guys think you're more serious about them than you are, and stop getting yourself hurt. There's nothing wrong with casual dating if it's what you want. You've just got to be clear with yourself about what you're really after, and go for that—not everything else!

Or, you have to take a long, hard look at yourself and realize that having such deep, emotional wounds that are clearly the barriers to your happiness might require the help of a professional. Figuring out what is behind your phobia of commitment will help you in the long run, and there's nothing wrong with seeking help to figure it out. The unavailable girl should, essentially, be gravitating towards the guys who gravitate towards her; the same way Monique should have been gravitating towards Paul.

What you want is someone who is dependable, who appreciates you, and who you can count on. When you gravitate towards men who are incapable of loving you, you just get yourself hurt.

Until you can find it in you to fix the barrier that is keeping you from having fulfilling relationships with healthy, loving guys, you are going to remain on the Unavailable Bitch hamster wheel!

CHAPTER 17:

Unrealistic Bitch

BEWARE OF YOUR EGO! The ego is a super villain, hell bent on destroying your sense of reality! Have you gone out with Gerard Butler lately? Is Johnny Depp still calling? No? Anything close? No? Hmmmmm, well, if you're holding out for that level of hotness and he NEVER shows up, you just might be in a delusional state, where you're listening to your self-sabotaging jerk of an ego a bit too much. Is it telling you, "You deserve the BEST. You deserve a rock star, a movie star, or the cutest guy on your block?" Damn that EGO! Woman, your eggs are rotting, and I think you just might be an Unrealistic Bitch!

❖ **Unrealistic Alert—Take the TEST!**

You might be an Unrealistic Bitch if:

- You're a 6, but you expect a 9—or even better, a 10.

- He has to be rich.
- He has to be tall (but you're short).
- He has to be smart (but you're no Mensa member).
- He has to be funny (but you're no laugh riot).
- He has to be in great shape (but you're not).
- He has to live in the best area of town (but you don't).
- He has to be childless.
- He can't have previously been married.
- He can only be three years younger or older than you.
- You are pushing 40, want to have a family (husband AND baby),yet HE still has to be super cute, super charming, tall, head full of hair, fit, smart and attracted to you—oh, and not too old.

So, how did you do on the test? Are you in touch with reality, or are you in need of a reality check?

Let's face it: when you're 80, you're not going to care if he ever had six-pack abs or if he was ever the sexiest guy in the room. So, with that in mind, think about what is really most important. If you're looking for a long-term, healthy relationship, then you have to look at "finding the one" from a new perspective.

�֍ Kate

Kate was 41, and she was constantly looking for Mr. Right. In fact, she had been looking for him her entire life, but she had never found him. Kate had been a cute, perky girl in her 20's, but even then, she was still just your average, cute, perky girl. She wasn't unattractive, but she never had "homecoming queen" looks.

Now at the age of 41, she had done really well with her career and had a great job as an attorney, which came with a lot of intense hours at work. She didn't have much free time to go to the gym or keep up with her appearance, and in the last five years, she had gained about 15 pounds.

Even with her demanding career, Kate never gave up hoping to get married and start a family. But, now her clock was TICKING VERY LOUD, and the sand was running out of the hourglass fast.

In order to hit the gas pedal about finding her future husband, she decided to try online dating. She posted two photos and filled out a profile. Right away, she was bombarded with emails from prospective dates. Unfortunately 95% of them she deleted right away, saying that they were either A) unattractive, B) overweight, or C) too old. But the 5% she chose were just her type: sexy and hot. In the first week of being on the site, she had three dates planned with three different guys. She had a brief phone chat with each of them, and she couldn't wait to meet them in person.

She came home from each date with a renewed sense of excitement. The guys she met were even better in person than she expected, and she couldn't wait to see them again. Each one of the guys at the end of the date said, "I'll call you!" But, they never did. Kate was devastated, especially when it kept happening, time and time again over the course of a month.

Finally, one of her friends said, "I met a great guy online, and we weren't a match because he wants to have a family and I don't. I think you guys would be a good match. You have a lot in common, and he's a down-to-earth, nice guy—very smart, and family oriented."

Kate took one look at his photo and immediately said, "No! No redheads."

His View

So why didn't the guys call from the online dating site that Kate liked so much? Well, let's let them tell you.

Rick: "When Kate walked into the restaurant, I didn't even recognize her. She walked up to me, and said, 'Hi!' I had to ask, 'Are you Kate?' Her pictures on the site had to have been at least 10 years old."

Greg: "I hate it when these chicks post old photos. They show up, and they aren't what they appeared to be online. She put down 'slim' on her profile, and she WAS NOT slim—not even close. It was a huge waste of my time."

Jeffrey: "Kate was nice, but she was not my type at all. In her photos, she looked fun, stylish and sexy, but when I met her, she was a little heavy, very little makeup, and kind of looked 'mom-ish.' She was nice enough, but I just wasn't attracted to her."

The Reality

Kate had posted old photos of herself and had included misleading information in her profile. Why? Maybe she still thought she looked like she did ten years ago, or maybe she, like many people, was completely oblivious to her own reality and was only concerned with what SHE wanted. Plus, what Kate was actively looking for is purely superficial! Superficial was not even in line with what she ultimately *needed* for the long term.

Kate thought she *needed* her future husband to be the cutest, sexiest, and most stylish guy. That's how she pre-qualified her candidates. But, why was it important that he be the cutest, most stylish, and sexiest guy out there? More importantly, was Kate aware that she herself was not the cutest, most stylish, sexiest GIRL out there? It should come as no surprise that guys that fit that criteria are looking for girls who fit that criteria as well.

Sadly, if Kate doesn't start opening her eyes to the reality that she's an average girl, who is overweight and racing the baby clock, she will miss the boat if she refuses to give up on her fantasy man. She is a smart girl with a lot to offer and that's what she needs to be looking for in a potential boyfriend and husband. Kate needs to be looking for a man that has long-term qualities and who would make a great, loyal husband and father.

There are many women out there who seem to have a false sense of entitlement when they are looking for love. We all need to be discerning and have standards, of course, but we also need to make sure that we are being honest with ourselves and that our standards aren't unrealistic. We need to make sure that we aren't asking for more than what we have to offer in return.

There are qualities you want in a potential partner. But do YOU have the same qualities to offer that person in return, or do you at least have something of equal value? Because, if your expectation is to date, marry or have a relationship with a "10," then my question to you is this: are you a "10?" Let's face it: if you're overweight, underweight, average looking, plain dressing, sweet but simple, smart but boring, or don't have a lot going for you other than you're a good person, well, let's just hope and pray that you're not waiting for "George Clooney" or "Brad Pitt" to come along.

This seems to be a very common problem with people who are over 35 and single. As you get older, you begin to get so set in your ways and stuck with very narrow and super specific criteria for a mate as your options get fewer and fewer. So obviously those criteria mean that the amount of dates you go on becomes less and less as well.

You're not getting any younger; you have fewer single friends; and you're also not going out as much as you once did. If you continue on the path of "no one is quite good enough," then I promise you that one morning, you are going to wake up and realize that the baby boat left the dock. Now, all of a sudden, you're 50 and alone.

What it comes down to is that when you're looking for a long-term partner, you need to evaluate the qualities you really want in someone long-term. This is someone you want to grow old with, right? Well, guess what? Hair turns gray, and six-pack abs give way to a few extra pounds as people get older. A great sense of style won't matter when he's 70. On the other hand, morals, intellect, compassion, and emotional connectivity will never go out of style. So, what you need to ask yourself when evaluating the qualities you want in a long-term partner is: "If everyone on this planet looked the same, dressed the same, had the same income, and was just as sexy as one another, what inner attributes would I be looking for?"

What are the qualities in a partner that would keep you fulfilled and happy fifty years from now? Is it important that he's smart, that he has similar interests to you, that he's creative, that he's funny, that he's crazy about you, and/or that he's completely devoted to you? Those are things that aren't going to go anywhere when he's 65, 75, or 85. And they're also things that you can probably find in a guy who's not a model.

Models are usually looking for models. 10's want 10's, 9's want 9's or 10's, 8's want 8's, 9's and 10's. Do you get my point here? Everyone wants that "10," so the line for that guy is around the block and down the street. Are you going to stand in line (with every other girl) and waste your time, or are you going be realistic and just go with what matters most: finding a good guy who will love you and appreciate you just the way you are.

CHAPTER 18:
The Bitches You Want To Be!

Now for the good news! Let's catch up with several of the women you met in the previous chapters. I'm sure you're wondering, what happened to that Momma Bitch after her boyfriend drove off into the sunset with Tiffany? And is Freaky Bitch still freaky? Is Unavailable Bitch still chasing men who don't want her? And poor Frumpy Bitch, was there any hope for her? Well, each of these women took a different path, and all had different results. I think you'll find their stories inspiring!

♥ *Sexy Bitch*

A Sexy Bitch is a woman who recognizes and embraces her feminine power. She isn't afraid to call attention to herself, and she enjoys playing up her flirty side. She is confident in her own skin, and she isn't intimidated by anyone.

Sandra

When we left off with Sandra (Frumpy Bitch), she was going on date after date with poor results. She was wearing unflattering clothes, and the feedback from her dates was that she was much less attractive than they expected and not nearly as pretty as she made herself seem on her online profile.

After several dates that Sandra set up online went nowhere, she decided to attend a speed-dating event with her sexy friend, Janna. Janna always got it right. She spent time getting ready and always wore the most flattering dress for the occasion. Sandra, on the other hand, wore—as you'd expect—her typical blah, "no effort" attire to the speed-dating event.

Sandra immediately picked up on the fact that with several of the guys that sat down to meet her, it was clear that none were interested in her. But, Janna, who was sitting at the next table over, was met with big smiles and fun conversation.

At the end of the event, Janna had given her number to several of the men, but Sandra came up empty.

As Janna and Sandra walked to their car, they overheard a few of the guys from the event discussing the ladies. "The blonde in the red dress? She was hot. Did you get her number? How about the one with the long, dark hair, in the black skirt? Wow!"

Then, one guy laughed and said, "Did you check out the mousy one with the baggy sweater? Yeah, loved her! Love the mom look!" The group of guys then all burst into laughter. Horrified, embarrassed, and suddenly very aware of her baggy sweater, Sandra got in the car with Janna, and she started to cry.

"What's wrong with me?" she said between sobs.

Janna put her hand on Sandra's back. "There is nothing wrong with you that a shopping trip can't fix! Sandra, I've been trying to tell you—you HAVE to start dressing sexier if you want to meet a guy! Look, you've ignored my advice all this time. Now, please, will you listen to me and let me take you shopping?"

Sandra, still crying, nodded. "Yes."

Janna said, "I know you're smart—so be smart enough to know that men like sexy women."

They both shared a giggle.

That weekend Janna and Sandra went on a shopping spree. At first, Sandra tried to fall back on her "comfort clothes," but Janna put her foot down. She then insisted that Sandra try on a few dresses that were fitted and sexy. One dress after another, Sandra began to feel sexy, and she realized that it was true. In the past, she really hadn't been putting much effort into her "look." She was ready to go with this new-and-improved Sandra and dive in all the way.

One day, on her way home from work, Sandra stopped at a salon, and when they were able to fit her in last minute, she went for highlights, a new hair cut, a manicure, and even got her eyebrows waxed.

With her new look, Sandra felt empowered and *beautiful*. She felt like she could walk into any room and have heads turn. She really liked that feeling. So, from that day forward, Sandra always put effort towards her appearance, even when she was just going to the grocery store. And guess what? Sandra's new approach to her appearance worked!

After posting new photos of herself (with her new look) on her online dating profile, Sandra set up quite a few dates—all of which were exciting. She was met with enthusiasm and most of the guys called her for a second and third date. She hit it off with one guy in particular: Dave. She and Dave have now been dating for six months, and everything is going great.

Sandra kicked it way up when she first started seeing Dave, and she caught his eye immediately. "My breath was taken away when she walked in the restaurant the first time we met. She was so pretty," reports Dave.

According to the couple, Sandra *does* let her hair down around Dave, who loves her more casual side too. Casual Sandra now is bounds sexier than Casual Sandra back in her frumpy days, though, and she's also oozing with confidence no matter what she's wearing. "To me, she's the total package: brains, beauty and confidence," says Dave.

♥ _Smart Bitch_

A Smart Bitch is a woman who learns from her mistakes, takes responsibility, and realizes all of her potential. She is unstoppable, resourceful, and fearless.

Stephanie

When we left off with Stephanie (Momma Bitch), she had just spent a lot of time and energy "improving" the life of her boyfriend, Mark. She moved him into her house; she nagged him until he got a job; and she upped his credit score. Mark grew to resent Stephanie, and ultimately, he left her for Tiffany.

After Mark left Stephanie, she was absolutely devastated. She had put so much into their relationship and had given so much of herself to Mark that she had all but lost track of who she was before the relationship. Moreover, although when Stephanie met Mark she had perfect credit, a full savings account, and a great group of friends, all of that went away the more she got involved with Mark. She was so intent on helping him "improve himself" that she put herself in debt cleaning up his messes. And as Stephanie had gotten deeper in her involvement with a guy her friends knew was bad for her, more and more distance had grown between her and her friends. When Mark left, Stephanie was left with a lot of debt and not a lot of emotional support.

Stephanie felt like she had hit rock bottom. How had this happened to her? And what was she going to do? Stephanie knew she had to focus on getting her life back on track, and one of the first steps she needed to take was to reconnect with her friends and then start getting herself out of debt.

Stephanie had always loved writing, and to earn some extra money, Stephanie applied for (and landed) a gig writing a relationship advice column for a local newspaper. Week after week, Stephanie found herself reading stories from women who had made big mistakes in life and love, just like she had. Stephanie felt a compassion for these women and committed herself to helping them get through their rough times by sharing her own experiences with them. Soon, in addition to writing her column, Stephanie moved on to coaching women on a private basis.

Stephanie got back on her feet in many ways, and in fact, today, she reports that she's in a much *better* place now than she was before she even met Mark. She mended many of her fractured relationships with her friends. She got back on top financially, and she found a new passion: helping other women make smart dating choices. Stephanie is still dating, but her entire life focus has changed. Now, she is committed to counseling and to helping the women she works with find their innermost potential. Nevertheless, Stephanie is such a strong, courageous, beautiful woman that when she does date, she has many great options to choose from. And her favorite mantra is: "The only boy I'm going to raise is the one I give birth to."

♥ *Sassy Bitch*

A Sassy Bitch is a woman who tests the limits but never crosses the line. She is the life of the party, but not a party girl. She's not afraid to be sexy and a little feisty.

She says what's on her mind and usually gets what she wants by playing it cool.

Sarah

When we left off with Sarah (Freaky Bitch), she had just tried to defy her friend Blake's insistence that he wasn't ready for a relationship by sleeping with him, thinking that sex would convert him from friend to boyfriend. Blake loved the sex, but he didn't throw away his conviction that he didn't want a relationship. Sarah was left alone and confused.

After Sarah's bad experience with Blake, she was hell bent on finding a boyfriend—and fast. Unfortunately, she didn't realize until much later that not only did sleeping with someone not magically turn him into a boyfriend overnight, but it also didn't set her up for any long-term relationships whatsoever.

Sarah got herself into a pattern: Go on a date. Sleep with a guy. Sleep with the guy again. Stop hearing from the guy. From there, she'd repeat it with another guy— and another.

Bored one night because she was between "dating" patterns, Sarah was clicking away on Facebook when she found herself on the page of Drew, a guy she had gone on a date (and subsequently slept with twice) a few weeks prior. He was cute, and she wished she'd gotten to see him again. Scrolling down his page to see what he had been up to, Sarah landed on a comment that caught her eye. A friend of Drew's had written on his page with this: "Hey, man, how was the date?"

Sarah checked when this had been posted, and lo-and-behold, it was just a few days after she and Drew had gone out for the first time! Beneath the wall post were two comments, which she eagerly read:

Drew wrote, "Oh, it was a GOOD time. She was VERY FUN!"

And the guy who had originally asked how it had gone, in reply, wrote "Hahaha—figured so."

Sarah was confused. What did this mean?

She had a friend who was mutual friends of both of the guys who had posted, so she gave the friend a call to see what was up.

Unfortunately, what the friend had to say was upsetting. "You'd dated another guy we know a few weeks back, and he had told all of us about the wild sex you guys had on the first date. Drew knew about how you had been with the other guy, and he kind of went in hoping you'd be the same with him."

"What do you mean, 'the same' with him?" Sarah asked.

The friend hesitated before saying, "Well, you know, not a challenge—*easy*, I guess?"

Mortified didn't begin to describe what Sarah experienced. Sure, Sarah had been having a lot of fun lately, but she never in a million years thought that she of all people would be labeled "easy." *After all,* she thought, *if a guy can have sex right away why couldn't she?*

Absolutely devastated and upset, she hung up the phone and began to cry. She wallowed in the realization that she was "easy" for a while before confiding in a close, loving friend: Melissa. "I never meant to be that way. I guess I just wasn't thinking," Sarah said to Melissa. Melissa and Sarah had a long talk that day, and they had several afterwards, too. Through self-reflection and talking to her friend, Sarah came to realize the difference between flirty, sexy, and being thought of as "fun," "easy," or "freaky." She could be flirty—even sassy—on the first date without jumping into bed with a guy. Showing him her true personality, which was really a sexy, sassy, and confident woman, allowed her to let the guys she went out with see her long-term potential, rather than her short-term freaky side. It was no mystery to guys that she dated that the fun, free, sassy spirited woman that she was on dates would likely translate to a good time in bed—when the time came.

Once she learned that she couldn't hand it all over on the first date and still expect there to be any real relationship potential, Sarah started to have a much more successful experience in the dating world. Several guys asked her out on multiple dates, and Sarah really took the time to get to know each of them. She particularly liked one guy, Dillon, and after seeing each other for a month and a half, they decided to become exclusive. Once they had decided they were exclusively with one another, it was still a couple of weeks before Sarah decided she was ready to have sex with Dillon for the first time. They did, and Sarah was really glad she waited.

"It might sound cheesy," said Sarah, "but even though you only lose your virginity once, the first time with someone who means a lot to you is really, really, special. I'm glad Dillon and I waited until we were involved to take that step. We were really starting to fall for one another, and that made it all the more wonderful when we were together that first time."

♥ *Married Bitch*

A Married Bitch is just that, married! Hitched, wedded, united, not single anymore! She found someone who loves and respects her and whom she also loves and respects. By being true to herself, she let down her guard and opened her heart to someone truly deserving.

Monique

When we left Monique (Unavailable Bitch), she had just broken up with yet another boyfriend, and she had lost the support and friendship of her good friend, Paul, who had been secretly pining after her for years.

Unfortunately, after Monique's breakup with Frank and her falling out with Paul, she continued on her self-destructive path. She went on to chase and subsequently date three more guys with whom it was never going to work out. First, there was Steve, a married out of town co-worker. Then, there was Bob, a bad boy bartender from a local bar, who was never exclusive to Monique, even though he said she was. (She caught him cheating *twice* before she ditched him, though.) Finally, there was Vince, the drug addict who was "working on himself" and trying to get over his addiction on his own. Their relationship came to an end when Monique found out that he had not only stolen money from family members to feed his addiction, but that he had also stolen from Monique.

After that final breakup, Monique felt like she had hit an ultimate low. Although Monique herself had been in denial about her own dating patterns for years, even she could see the writing beginning to finally form on the wall. "Why would I get involved with a guy I knew had a drug problem and then be surprised when it didn't work out? What is *my* problem?"

One major issue was that Monique didn't know what her problem was. Feeling helpless and unsure of what she could possibly do to fix herself, Monique did a wise thing and sought the help of a therapist. On her first visit to the therapist, when the doctor asked her what had brought her to the point where she decided she wanted help, Monique said, "I just had a particularly weird and bad breakup, and it made me realize I've been dating men for years where it didn't work out. It never works out. I'm starting to worry that the problem is me."

With the help of her therapist, Monique came to understand and accept that indeed she was the one standing in the way of herself and healthy relationships. There were emotional scars that Monique had from her past that were keeping Monique from embracing the idea of commitment to or from someone else. She had wounds that needed to heal before she could expect to give or receive love in a normal way. All of those years, she had been closing herself off because she had demons that were making her unavailable. It took really facing that fact and working with her therapist to work through those issues to become emotionally sound and available in a real way.

(I saved the best story for last, because this one actually has *two* happy endings within it.) After Monique did a lot of work on healing herself, she realized through talking with her therapist that in her period of unavailable dating, she had alienated someone who was very important in her life: Paul. He had always been there for her, and she never took his advice. In fact, she often trampled all over his advice by defying it. It was no surprise that Paul eventually had to leave their friendship to preserve his own feelings.

Monique went to Paul and apologized to him, and let him know what she was going through and what she was doing to change. Paul, meanwhile, had been dating someone, but that relationship had recently ended. Now with his and Monique's relationship on the mend, he started to see the vibrant, great girl he had once had eyes for. The best part was, this time around, Monique returned those feelings.

Monique and Paul's friendship grew stronger and stronger until eventually, Monique asked Paul out on a date, and he happily said yes.

They soon entered into a stable, loving relationship, and after a year of two best friends falling deeply in love, Paul asked Monique to marry him. She said yes, and they had a very romantic and beautiful wedding.

For Monique, Paul, and, yes, even you, there really is such a thing as happily ever after!

FROM ME TO YOU:
A Note from the Author

I hope you enjoyed reading the book, and I hope you learned a few things along the way. But, the most important lesson is that life is about balance. You go too far in one direction, and you're obsessive. You go too far in the other, and you're self-centered. On a sliding scale, at one end, you're too picky, and at the other end, you're too easy. Again, life is about balance. You don't want to be that person who goes on a date and talks the entire time about yourself, and you don't want to be the person who grills your date like you're an FBI investigator.

The people that I have observed who remain single for long periods of time are those people who are usually always at one end or the other, but they are rarely balanced and in the middle. In order to have a relationship, you have to be in the middle; otherwise, you can never meet someone half way.

So, if some of the stories I shared with you seemed like the men could do no wrong, know that is not the case. Men are wrong as much as we are! And, yes, there are those men who will make you feel more insecure than others and will take advantage of you if they know they can. While these guys might try (consciously or unconsciously) to bring out the worst in you, it is only you that can allow it to happen. Your mind controls everything you do, so no one but you can make you do anything that you don't want to do. You teach people how to treat you, and you show people who you are by your actions.

I'm sure we've all been irrational, picky, self-centered, unavailable, frumpy, obsessive, freaky, bitter, all business, unrealistic, a pain in the ass, insecure, needy, a momma, bossy and even dumb at times—and they're all fine in small doses. However, what I hope you learned from this book is that being too much of any one of these will limit your options and will keep you from being in a great relationship. Quite frankly, all of these behaviors will really get you nowhere but alone in the end—and I don't want you to be alone!

Life is meant to be shared and enjoyed with other people. So take a deep breath, open your mind, and stop doing all of those things that you do that have prevented you from finding love. Even if it means just one day a week, try to do something different than you would normally do. I recommend testing your limits and your courage every day. If you are at your best and you are mentally and emotionally the healthiest you can be, then you will absolutely find love, or even better, love will find you.

~ Gina Hendrix

ABOUT THE AUTHOR

Gina Hendrix is many things to many people. To her clients, she is a concierge matchmaker, matching the most sought after bachelors with the most beautiful and interesting women. To many single women she is a coach, mentor and inspiration. To animals, she is a best friend and advocate. To the rest of the world, she is a straight shooting, no nonsense person, willing to help anyone in need of advice and guidance.

Gina has been a featured guest speaker at The Learning Annex, Pepperdine University, and at many seminars across the country. She has been seen on E! and the Lifetime Network. Many people will remember Gina from her very popular show Love Life Makeovers. She currently has a new radio show called Beyond Beautiful on Latalkradio.com, where she has candid conversations with the world's most beautiful and intriguing people about life, love and the pursuit of happiness.

"I love helping people in every way and with my company Exclusive Introductions and now my show Beyond Beautiful, I can help people enrich their lives on so many levels, it is absolutely the most rewarding thing I have ever done."

For more information on Gina please visit her website: Exclusiveinla.com

Made in the USA
Las Vegas, NV
03 November 2021